GUE[illegible]A GO[illegible]PEL

READING THE BIBLE FOR LIBERATION
IN THE POWER OF THE SPIRIT

FOREWORD BY GERALD O. WEST

BOB EKBLAD

THE PEOPLE'S SEMINARY PRESS

Guerrilla Gospel
Reading the Bible for Liberation in the Power of the Spirit

The People's Seminary Press
P.O. BOX 410
Burlington, WA 98233
www.peoplesseminary.org

ISBN: 978-1-5466-7136-7

Made in the USA.

TABLE OF CONTENTS

ACKNOWLEDGMENTS

Special thanks to the following people for their help on this book. The inmates of Skagit County Jail and Washington State Reformatory have been my most regular reading companions and fellow witnesses of Jesus' revolutionary love. Our Tierra Nueva staff, fellow jail chaplains and worshipping community participants have also contributed insights that have made their way into this book. Karen Hollenbeck-Wuest helped me with valuable editing, expert advice and encouragement. Pauline Hoggarth, Roger Wilkinson, John Boggis and Martin and Alison Robinson each read earlier versions of this book, offering me valuable comments and corrections. Roger Capron, Mike Neelley, Brad Jersak, Lucy Peppiatt, Matt Lynch and John Hall also offered helpful observations and encouragement during the writing process. Conversations and Bible studies with David Calix, Julio Montalvo, Salvio Hernandez, Jessica Cargill and Lucrezia Bush directly influenced many of these chapters. Thanks to Roswell Cho for ideas regarding the book title, Jim LePage for designing the cover with great skill and creativity, and Vicki Frye for her expertise at layout. Gerald West's Bible study facilitation, teaching, writing and friendship have been an inspiring influence for years.

My wife Gracie's devotion to Jesus and love for Scripture are contagious. Her love and companionship in life and ministry are constant. I look forward to many more years of friendship, adventure and guerrilla gospel encounters with her.

Thanks be to God, for constant love, support, and inspiration through the Holy Spirit, and Jesus' example and forever impactful teaching in the beautiful Gospels.

FOREWORD

GERALD O. WEST

"Many people have experienced the Bible as a weapon used against them by people in power," Bob Ekblad begins his third chapter on a liberating reading of the Bible. For the poor and marginalised, the Bible is often bad news rather than the good news that Jesus came to proclaim to "the poor": "to proclaim release to the captives, the recovery of sight to the blind, to set free the oppressed, to proclaim the favourable year of the Lord" (Luke 4:18–19).

This is Bob Ekblad's startling summons to the guerrilla activity that Jesus enlists us to live out and proclaim. The profound recognition that what should be good news is so often bad news is Bob's gift of insight to Christians. An HIV-positive young woman is told by her pastor that she should not touch the Bible because she is unclean. An unemployed young man is told by his Christian family that his unemployment is a punishment from God for his sinfulness. A disabled child is left at home while her family goes to church because her failure to be healed brings shame on the family. A faithful Sunday School teacher is told to give up her ministry because she is lesbian. A woman who is serially abused by her husband is instructed by her pastor to continue to submit to him. In each and every case, the Bible is used to proclaim this bad news. But what, Bob asks, if the Bible is really good news for the poor and marginalised?

For the Bible to be good news, Bob argues, it must be released from its domestication. We must humble ourselves before the unruly guerrilla detail of Scripture. We must resist the dominant and dominating notion that the Bible is about moralism. We must resist our propensity to focus on the heroic dimensions of biblical characters without recognising their fallibility and failures. Indeed, Bob sees the divine proclamation of good news in the very ordinariness of biblical narrative.

I remember well a Bible study Bob led in the local jail near his home when he asked the inmates about their images of God. The recurring image was of a powerful figure who used surveillance to control, shame, and punish. God was like the prison guards, the border officials, the judge. The group then read a well-known gospel story where the Pharisees use Scripture to stigmatise and marginalise and then are confronted by Jesus, who always stands in solidarity with the one being stigmatised and marginalised and uses the very same Scriptures to affirm and include. "Who in this gospel story," Bob asked the inmates, "is like the God you have imagined, Jesus or the Pharisees?" The inmates were unanimous, "the Pharisees." For the next twenty minutes, we all participated in a dialogical, guerrilla rereading of the Bible. By the time the prison guards came to fetch the inmates, we had concluded that if Jesus is the truest and fullest representation of God, we must reimagine God to be liberative, inclusive, and compassionate. I have never forgotten this encounter, for many years later I watched with horror as South Africans living with HIV were told by their churches that AIDS was a punishment from God, the wages of sin. Fortunately I had Bob Ekblad's example to draw on, and so we returned to the very same gospel stories in which Jesus offers a redeeming and healing—rather than a condemning and destroying—image of God.

If we truly believe that the Bible is good news, we will be shaken from our passivity and compelled to collaborate with Comandante Jésus, joining him in a compassionate yet militant guerrilla interpretation of the Bible. Bob provides us with the subversive and revolutionary theological orientations that we need to go about this.

He also offers us a model for how we can participate in the guerrilla gospel by contextualizing the "See-Judge-Act" process, which becomes seeing, discerning, and responding. Trained as a biblical scholar, Bob offers a rereading of Scripture, but much of the book is about *seeing* the reality of our world. Over the many years of his ministry, Bob Ekblad has deepened his understanding of what it means to *see* reality. An analytical understanding of the social, cultural, economic, political, and religious systems that dominate and oppress the poor and marginalised have been central to his vocation. In recent years, he has become more attentive to the individual affective domains of life, allowing the Spirit to reveal dimensions of reality that cannot readily be explained by systemic analysis. What might be called "spiritual discernment" has come to play an important role in his recognition of the signs of our times, whether communal or individual.

Because the guerrilla gospel speaks into reality in all its complexity, Bob says that preparing guerrilla Bible studies requires "meditation, prayer, and study." Because guerrilla work is so overtly activist, subversive, and revolutionary, it can often be misunderstood as delinked from the ordinary life of faith familiar to most believers. Bob makes it clear that guerrilla Bible studies find their formation in the ordinariness of faith. They are subversive and revolutionary, but only because our Christian faith, as portrayed and proclaimed by Jesus, is subversive and revolutionary.

"Asking the Spirit for wisdom, inspiration, and revelation" is vital to the preparation of guerrilla Bible studies, but so is the hard work of focussing on the detail of Scripture, where God—not the devil— is found. Yet much of the detail of Scripture is not recognised or read because we have domesticated the Bible, allowing our predetermined theological orientations to guide what we see and hear in Scripture. Bob shares his considerable experience as a socially engaged scholar and practitioner of the guerrilla art of rereading Scripture to open us to a "slow" reading of Scripture so that the Spirit can disrupt our well-worn theologies of moralism.

One of the signs of our religious times is that church leadership has become more and more autocratic, dominated by celebrity "men of God." Ordinary Christians, as Bob reminds us, have become increasingly passive, receivers of blessing rather than sharers of blessing. Guerrilla gospel encounters require active facilitation skills because they require active participation. My enduring memory of Bob is watching him facilitate participation, even in the most unlikely places, such as with inmates in jail or migrant fruit pickers in a farmer's field. Facilitation is an art, skill, and spiritual discipline. This book devotes considerable space to offering resources for us all to become better facilitators.

Guerrilla Bible studies are not about knowing our Bibles better, though they will deepen our understanding of Scripture, but rather changing our realities, both social and individual. True to See-Judge-Act praxis, we engage in guerrilla Bible studies to "bring about conversion, healing, and personal and social transformation," as Bob says. Guerrilla Bible studies are about changing our realities, social and individual. We change in the very process of participating in a guerrilla Bible study and the guerrilla Bible study equips us with resources with which we can work with God in transforming our world.

This book is a valuable resource for all who yearn to participate in God's subversive and revolutionary work. Bob offers anecdotes from his decades of experience in diverse contexts that embody guerrilla interpretation, for they are the flesh and blood of the guerrilla gospel.

PREFACE

Jesus of Nazareth is my inspiration for life and ministry, and what I call "Bible studies" or "guerrilla gospel encounters." Through his life and teaching recorded in the Gospels of the New Testament, he defines the word gospel, which means good news or liberating message. According to New Testament Scriptures, Jesus is God's Son, Israel's Messiah, and the Lord himself in the flesh. He was born into a world marked by oppression and injustice to announce and embody God's global liberation movement. Like an insurgent, Jesus comes in under the radar, behind enemy lines, and then builds a foundation of trust with a growing entourage of humble followers. He resists the authorities of his day, along with their legal systems, and he calls others to join him.

Jesus incites a revolution that he calls the Kingdom of God. He starts out incognito, but after his baptism at age thirty, he publicly demonstrates an unprecedented authority in his teaching, which is backed up by acts of healing, advocacy, and liberation on behalf of the oppressed, poor, or disenfranchised. In Jesus' many encounters in the Gospels, he breaks the established rules to advocate for the marginalized. He confronts the powers—both visible and invisible, modeling a holistic spiritual warfare that brings freedom.

I am compelled by the way he loves people so freely and effectively wherever he goes, seeking and finding the lost and forsaken, raising up the downtrodden and hopeless, offering abundant life to all who will follow him. Reading about Jesus in the Gospels inspires me to follow him, to go deep with him, to tune into his instructions in my daily life, and to work with him to reach others with the good news he embodies and proclaims throughout the New Testament.

This book begins with an overview of what I'm calling the guerrilla gospel—the liberating message found in Scripture, most clearly visible in Jesus of Nazareth's life and teaching as portrayed in the New Testament. Included in this book are perspectives and suggestions about how to receive and prepare messages that invite conversion, inciting liberating action and engendering healing and holistic transformation. A major focus of this book is to offer practical ways to facilitate conversation around the Bible in marginal settings, with people who are not accustomed to being personally met, loved, and called by God. Whether among prison inmates, impoverished urban slum dwellers, African villagers, educated or uneducated Westerners, or regular church-goers, my hope is to facilitate life-transforming encounters mediated through dialogical reflection on Scripture.

I wrote this book twelve years after *Reading the Bible with the Damned,*[1] my first attempt to communicate this way of reading the Bible with people on the margins. At that time, my focus was on economic and social margins and those who were experiencing exclusion from the mainstream or dominant culture. Though I continue to prioritize reading Scripture as good news amongst the poor and excluded, I also see that the good news discovered amongst prisoners, drug users, and gang members can ignite the hearts of those in more ordinary or mainstream circles who've found the Bible dull, unrelated to their lives, or foreign and problematic. I am convinced that reading the Bible can feed our faith and inspire liberating action that will bring about personal and social transformation.

My approach and theology have continued to be purified by the fires of life and ministry. Over the past twelve years, I have searched the global body of Christ and the alleyways and hedges of the biblical canon for good news that has the power to transform lives. This pursuit has hastened as I have continued to see some of our most beloved and inspired inmates, farm workers, and Honduran peasant Bible study participants relapse, re-offend, or succumb to the seductions and idols of our age. Others have stepped into greater health and become active in ministry. My pursuit of fruitful approaches has also led me to cross lines of difference, humbly learning from ministers and practitioners from divergent camps.

1. Bob Ekblad, *Reading the Bible with the Damned,* (Louisville: Westminster John Knox, 2005).

PREFACE

Guerrilla Gospel: Reading the Bible for Liberation in the Power of the Spirit is a "training" manual that I hope will help readers envision the scope of Jesus' revolution and how we can more fully participate in it. Part one is designed to help readers prepare Bible studies. Chapter 1 presents Jesus' insurgent movement; chapter 2 identifies assumptions underlying liberating readings of Scripture; chapter 3 outlines the larger mission of God in Scripture; chapter 4 presents a case study of Jesus' encounter with one individual and her community.

Part two focuses on facilitating Bible studies, (AKA guerrilla gospel encounters). Chapter 5 considers how we can see in alignment with Jesus' vision; chapter 6 identifies how to hear and perceive prophetic revelation; chapter 7 discusses how to prepare liberating messages; chapter 8 focuses on how to facilitate Bible studies in diverse settings; chapter 9 explores how to employ the gifts of the Spirit as "guerrilla tactics" while leading Bible studies, preaching, or teaching.

PART I:

PREPARING GUERRILLA GOSPEL ENCOUNTERS

CHAPTER ONE

FOLLOWING COMANDANTE JÉSUS

I joke with former gang members involved in Tierra Nueva's ministry about how Jesus is our *comandante,* which is Spanish for military or guerrilla commander. He's the one who calls the shots, instructing soldier disciples in the trenches of warfare to advance the movement as an unprecedented and truly life-giving insurgency, to win over inhabitants, neighborhoods and people groups of the world for the kingdom of God. These friends are used to gang shot-callers or are themselves shot-callers. But they are tired of living in fear, grieving beloved homies[2] killed in drive-by shootings, and spending years of their lives serving long prison sentences. We love that Jesus is an outsider, on the hunt for recruits, eager to go out on missions. We love that he gathers with his confidants in the mountains or in boats, on foot or on the move from town-to-town, stopping along roadsides, visiting people in homes, teaching and healing crowds along the way in fields or synagogues, on beaches or in the wilderness.

Talking like this about Jesus gets us excited. We've all seen too many casualties of the fast life of both legal and illegal workaholism, drugs, alcohol, and poverty, gang violence and domestic violence. We've had enough of relationship breakdown, children taken by Child Protective Services, incarceration, premature death by suicide, homicide, overdose, and different illnesses. Many of us know firsthand the life-restoring benefits of Jesus' saving help and want to see others benefit too. Being part of a

2. "Homies" is gang slang, short for "homeboys"—meaning fellow gang members from the same neighborhood.

movement of true liberation compels us, giving us a new reason to live—and perhaps even something to die for.

The dictionary definition for "guerrilla" works to a certain extent to describe Jesus and his followers, past and present: "a member of a band of irregular soldiers that uses guerrilla warfare, harassing the enemy by surprise raids, sabotaging communication and supply lines."[3] In Spanish, *guerrilla* is the diminutive for *guerra* (war), which includes the notion of small-scale war. Guerrilla warfare is defined as "the use of hit-and-run tactics by small, mobile groups of irregular forces operating in territory controlled by a hostile, regular force." The ministry of Jesus is all about reaching and empowering ordinary people and usually involves prolonged struggle against formidable powers. It requires flexibility, adaptability, and being on-point around the clock.

Unlike modern guerrilla warfare, Jesus refuses physical violence, coercion, and terror (Mt 26:52; Lk 9:55). But like guerrilla activity, Jesus uses unconventional tactics, travels in small, mobile bands (Mk 9:30), recruits from among the outcasts (Mk 2:15), advocates for the oppressed (Lk 13:16), depends on local collaborators for support (Lk 8:3; Jn 12:1-2), and multiplies his followers and thereby his fighting force (Lk 10:1).

There's a subversive dimension of Jesus' presence as God infiltrates the human race. God's strategy is to be born undercover, behind enemy lines, into a family that is both humble and yet has ties to the people's hero, King David. Jesus, though, takes the revolution to a new level. Jesus' first thirty years as a carpenter in Nazareth reveal how keen God is about sleeper-cell beginnings as a way to imbed his yeast-like realm outside the radar of empire. Once activated at his baptism, Jesus embodies an unprecedented authority that attracts adherents, and the movement multiplies amongst the disenfranchised.

Jesus' main way of operating is to meet up with people wherever he finds them. He is not a commander who runs things from a safe distance, but an on-the-ground, front-line activist. He often takes the initiative, going after people personally. He sees and calls ordinary people—fishermen (Mt 4:18–22) and tax collectors (Mt 9:9), including the chief tax-collector, Zaccheus, whom he calls down from a tree, and then invites

3. Dictionary.com.

himself to his house for a stay (Lk 19:1–10). Jesus sees a man paralyzed for thirty-eight years among invalids at a sheep gate, asks him if he wants to be well, and then heals him on the spot (Jn 5:2–9). Jesus also attracts adherents from among more privileged sectors: the Pharisee leader, Nicodemus, who is impressed by his signs (Jn 3:1–2); Joanna, the wife of Herod's steward, Chuza who supports Jesus and the disciples financially; (Lk 8:3) a synagogue official who is desperate to see his dying daughter healed (Lk 8:41); a Roman centurion who begs Jesus to heal his slave (Mt 8:5–9). Are you ready to join up?

Other times, Jesus' encounters are a bit on the fly, unplanned meetings that seem to be interruptions. Blind people and lepers cry to him for mercy from the roadsides, and he stops to heal or cleanse, teaching as he goes (see Lk 18:35–43; Mk 10:46–52; Mt 8:1–3). People also come to Jesus with the need for deliverance (e.g., Mt 8:16, 9:32–33; Mk 5:2–16). In every case, these encounters become opportunities for Jesus to teach, challenge, and offer immediate relief. In one instance, men cut a hole in the roof and lower a paralyzed man down in front of Jesus and some antagonistic religious leaders, and Jesus spontaneously declares to the paralytic, "your sins are forgiven" (Mk 2:2–7). Then Jesus proves his authority by telling the man to "rise, take up your pallet and go home" (Mk 2:8–11). Such actions inspire discussion and sometimes aggression from Jesus' enemies.

Jesus often uses the language of guerrilla warfare in his instructions to his disciples, and there's a combativeness to his words and actions throughout the Gospels. "Behold, I have given you authority to tread on serpents and scorpions, and over all the power of the enemy, and nothing will injure you," Jesus instructs seventy of his fresh recruits (Lk 10:19). He also proclaims violence against unseen enemies: "The Son of God appeared for this purpose, to destroy the works of the devil" (1 Jn 3:8). Since "the whole world lies in the power of the evil one," Jesus and his disciples must organize a strike force and be adequately equipped for the task (1 Jn 5:18).

Jesus also uses kingdom tactics and an arsenal of weapons that are "not of this world" (Jn 18:36), such as prayer, fasting, forgiveness, love, and the power of God. His armory also includes words, which he and his disciples wield as an integral part of their mission to announce the good news to all of creation (Mk 16:15). Jesus himself says: "Do not think that I came to bring peace on the earth; I did not come to bring peace, but a sword" (Mt 10:34). This sword is elsewhere called "the sword of the Spirit" and is equated with the Word of God (Eph 6:17) as part of the believers' arsenal (Eph 6:13-17). Hebrews 4:12 states this clearly: "For the word of God is living and active and sharper than any two-edged sword." Jesus even drives out evil spirits with a word (Mt 8:16).

Jesus' ministry of the Word includes teaching, preaching, healing, deliverance, and prophecy. Jesus commands his disciples: "Preach, saying, 'The kingdom of heaven is at hand.' Heal the sick, raise the dead, cleanse the lepers, cast out demons. Freely you received, freely give" (Mt 10:7–8). All these actions and others too are part of Jesus' weaponry. Physical violence is never included in Jesus' tactics—but rather active enemy love. This love includes the resistance of evil and injustice through exposure and verbal confrontation as well as public non-compliance with unjust laws.

Throughout Jesus' earthly ministry, he is neither a religious nor social insider, but operates outside the circles of Jewish religious organizations and certainly of the Roman Empire. He does not enjoy elevated status within a religion collaborating with the powers, nor is he an accepted leader by the dominant culture. Rather, he lives outside an overarching theocracy, and the kingdom he proclaims is decidedly "not of this world" (Jn 18:36). In fact, in a subversive analogy he compares himself to a thief who comes to burglarize a house (Mt 24:43; Lk 12:39), first tying up the strong man before robbing his goods (Mt 12:29; Mk 3:27). This imagery suggests that the world is like a prison, which implies that Jesus' mission—and therefore ours—is to engage in prison breaks that will liberate captives rather than reform and take over the prison! Jesus even commissions Peter as head of a movement called church to storm the gates of hell to free captives (Mat 16:18).

Unlike contemporary religions and political ideologies that seek to increase control and domination, Jesus doesn't call his followers to take up arms in a combatant way to prevent or defend against the kingdoms of this world (Mt 20:25-26). In fact, Jesus rebukes his disciples for trying to defend him with weapons, saying: "Do you think that I cannot appeal to my Father, and he will at once put at my disposal more than twelve legions of angels?" (Mt 26:53).

Jesus describes himself as "from above" (Jn 3:31) in contrast to everyone else "from below," (Jn 8:23) and tells his contemporaries that he will soon leave to a place where they can't find him (Jn 7:34–36). From his rightful place in this kingdom, he informs us of heaven's priorities so that we can embody his "on earth as in heaven" agenda (Mt 6:10). Today, in our increasingly post-Christendom world, we must deliberately own our "aliens and strangers" status (1 Pt 1:1, 2:11) by fully embracing our heavenly "no longer strangers and aliens" identity (Eph 2:19). As you follow Jesus, an identity shift happens that will put you at odds with the culture and dominant values around you, leading others to possibly view you as a kind of resister. Jesus describes himself as one who is rejected (Jn 12:48), hated (Jn 7:7, 15:18, 23, 24, 25), and persecuted (Jn 15:20). He promises his followers that they will experience these things as well,[4] as he includes them as "not of the world" (Jn 17:14).

In contrast to guerrilla combatants who operate in secrecy, sneaking around the powerful state, Jesus mostly speaks and acts openly in public settings. He teaches in synagogues and in the Jerusalem temple, overturning the tables of money-changers and directly confronting religious leaders (Mt 21:12-13). "I have spoken openly to the world; I always taught in synagogues and in the temple, where all the Jews come together; and I spoke nothing in secret," Jesus tells Pilate (Jn 18:20). Jesus considers the temple his Father's house (Lk 2:49) and recognizes that "the earth is the Lord's" (Ps 24:1). Yet when Jewish leaders plot Jesus' death, he stops moving about in Judea and limits his walking to Galilee (Jn 7:1). When temple leaders in Jerusalem pick up stones to throw at Jesus, he hides himself (Jn 8:59). When they try to seize him, he eludes "their grasp" (Jn 10:39). When Jewish authorities begin planning together to kill him, "he no longer" continues "to walk publicly," but goes "away from there to the country near the wilderness" (Jn 11:54). The fact that chief priests and Pharisees order the people to inform them about Jesus' whereabouts in order to arrest him marks Jesus as a subversive troublemaker who must

4. See Matthew 10:22; 24:9; Luke 6:22; 21:12,, 17; John 15:18–19, 20; 17:14.

take precautions (see Jn 11:57). So does the fact that he is eventually crucified between two criminals (Lk 23:32).

Jesus' public ministry only lasts three years before he is arrested and executed as a law-breaker by crucifixion. In that short time, Jesus focuses on living out his Father's mission. He recruits twelve disciples, who travel with him everywhere, receiving his teaching and witnessing his direct action. Eleven of these disciples are among the 120 who receive the Holy Spirit at Pentecost. Jesus' explosive life inspires a movement of followers, who—after being empowered by the Holy Spirit at Pentecost—continue to embody and proclaim the kingdom of God.

The life and teachings of Jesus fulfill God's historic mission to save the world and set the bar for action until he returns. Jesus' many encounters with people are written up in the New Testament Scriptures to be read and discussed today, inviting and inspiring us towards Christ-like action. Our task is to figure out how we can transmit his rich teaching in similar places on behalf of similar beneficiaries—how we can "get away with a Bible study," as I'm fond of saying—or with a guerrilla gospel encounter.

The Gospels' presentations of Jesus' life and teachings as Israel's Messiah are preceded by the Old Testament Scriptures, which include material that depicts God in ways that seem out of alignment with Jesus. Accounts of God's judgment of sinners, laws requiring sacrifice of animals, the separation of unclean from clean people, and graphic depictions of violent conquest of the Canaanites can bring confusion to Bible readers hunting for good news. In the next chapter we will identify pitfalls to avoid and assumptions to consider for reading the Bible for liberation now. In chapter three we will then consider some possible ways to look at the larger story of Scripture in alignment with the revelation of God in Jesus, before focusing more closely on how he engages in a guerrilla gospel encounter with a Samaritan woman in chapter four.

CHAPTER TWO

ASSUMPTIONS FOR A LIBERATING READING OF THE BIBLE

Many people have experienced the Bible as a weapon used against them by people in power—parents, teachers, evangelists, pastors, priests, missionaries, employers, and even judges and government officials. In Spanish the word *sermon* is synonymous for a scolding. In rural Central America, *la biblia* is a Spanish slang term for machete, which peasants carry unsheathed as both a weapon for self-defense and a tool. Many people avoid reading the Bible because they are afraid they will discover God's charges against them along with God's sentence for sins they have committed.

Even people outside the church have heard of Old Testament laws condemning rebellious children, adulterers, homosexuals, and many other transgressors to death. They may also be familiar with New Testaments texts used to silence women, justify slavery, and demand subservience to oppressive governments. Most have heard about the drowning of people and animals in the Flood (Gn 7:21-23)), and of fire and brimstone raining down from heaven on the ungodly in Sodom and Gomorrah (Gn 19:24). Many people are familiar with the stories of Israel's violent conquest of the land of Canaan and God's commands to dislocate or completely destroy the local inhabitants, including men, women, children, and animals.[5] Catholic and Protestant colonizers from Western nations have taken land and massacred, imprisoned, and enslaved its people, using the Bible to justify their exploits. In North America, Christian settlers massacred and dispossessed First Nations and Native Americans, forcing them onto reservations or into residential schools, where they were forced to read the Bible and abandon their native religions.

More recently, Christian endorsement of wars, conservative moral issues, and political candidates who promote policies that hurt the poor, immigrants, and the environment and who support defense spending and military interventions has engendered associations between Christians, the Bible, and legalistic, judgmental, racist, and violent attitudes. Those growing up in Christian homes who have suffered abuse, neglect, or marital strife may have seen Scripture used to justify such destructive attitudes or actions and will likely have negative views about God, the Christian faith, and the Bible.[6]

When you read the Bible with people suffering from poverty, social exclusion, or oppression, you quickly learn that these widespread negative prejudices—in society at-large and also inside the church—must be addressed before the good news can be heard. Your awareness of people's past history with the Bible and Christian faith will help you understand the many pitfalls in reading the Bible for liberation. Some common pitfalls will be discussed in the next section. Then I will outline some positive theological assumptions that will help frame a liberatory reading of Scripture.

5. I will not attempt to interpret these difficult texts in this book, but I plan to do so in a forthcoming book. For some helpful perspectives on these texts and many others, see Gregory A. Boyd, *Crucifixion of the Warrior God: Interpreting the Old Testament Violent Portraits of God in Light of the Cross*, 2 vols. (Minneapolis: Fortress, 2017) and Derek Flood, *Disarming Scripture: Cherry-Picking Liberals, Violence-Loving Conservatives, and Why We All Need to Read the Bible Like Jesus Did* (San Francisco: Metanoia Books, 2014).

6. See Simone Pacot's helpful discussion on common familiar origins of negative images of God in *Evangelizing the Depths*, (Eugene: Cascade Books, 2018), 17-23.

PITFALLS TO LIBERATORY READING OF SCRIPTURE

Pitfalls are prejudices or negative assumptions that people assume are true unless directly countered with a convincing positive alternative. Following are some common pitfalls to reading the Bible for liberation, which I have identified in many places throughout the world.

Expecting Bad News

The pitfall of expecting bad news from Scripture comes from people's experiences in religious environments that are rife with judgment and exclusion. When reading or listening to the Bible, many people brace themselves for condemnation or, at best, bitter medicine, rather than anticipating life-giving messages of comfort, relief, and inspiration. Jail inmates have often told me that they have avoided reading the Bible for years, because they expected to find descriptions of punishments awaiting them for their sins.

Further reflection: Have you experienced this pitfall yourself or witnessed this amongst people you read with?

Domestication

The Bible is domesticated when we dismiss, explain away, or ignore direct challenges or difficulties that we encounter when interpreting Scripture. When we read alone or in circles of sameness, we often reinforce interpretations with which we are comfortable. As human beings we naturally long for community, acceptance, and encouragement. We are drawn to people of similar mind and values. Though there's nothing inherently wrong with this, our attraction to likeness often leads us into circles marked by relative uniformity in terms of race, nationality, social class, theology, and political views. When we limit our reading of the Bible to circles of sameness, our views will not be challenged, and we will tend to interpret along the lines of our community. An internal censor that dismisses alternate viewpoints can operate unconsciously, so that our interpretations align with the respected authorities in our circles. Often our beliefs about what God can and will do in our lives and world are limited by the lived experience of people in our group, leading to group-aligned expectations of God, which may be quite low depending on people's experiences. Domestication blocks us from being open to new perspectives, revelations, and experiences of God. Domestication also holds us back from hearing and receiving a fresh word from Scripture or Bible study participants, which can also lead to boredom and indifference.

Remedies for domestication include deliberately exposing ourselves to different ideas and people through education, travel, and relationships outside of our subcultures, church, and country and letting the breadth of Scripture challenge our assumptions.

Further reflection: What steps do you feel inspired to take to broaden your reading community?

Moralism

Moralism is an orientation towards life that focuses on knowing the right answers and rules and then seeking to live by them. From this perspective, the Bible provides answers and rules for a successful life in this world and entry into heaven. The rich young ruler's question to Jesus, "what must I do to be saved?" epitomizes those who are caught up in this mindset. While this question is not negative in itself, it often assumes that God is a cosmic employer, judge, or police officer, ready to demote or punish people for bad behavior and reward them for good performance. Fear of failure, condemnation, and damnation by God usually underlie religious moralism. Performance-oriented interpretation looks for the right beliefs and actions that will lead to divine approval. These answers can be conservative or liberal, depending on one's values.

A desire to please God is certainly right and good. The problem comes when we think we can save ourselves through our thinking and behavior, which leads to a performance-based orientation, slavery to rules, "us-them" thinking regarding those who do not live up to the determined standards, and endless striving to meet the demands of perfectionism. Compliance with values, principles, or laws is prioritized over faith in God's salvation and gift of life by grace. After all, "we are justified by faith in Christ and not by the works of the law" (Gal 2:16).

Further reflection: Do you notice moralistic Bible reading tendencies in yourself or in others around you? What has helped you read Scripture in ways that inspire rather than guilt you into redemptive action?

Heroism

Heroism is the tendency to identify exemplary characters or saints in Scripture after whom we can model our lives. Because of the widespread influence of moralism, many people assume that the Bible presents exemplary, heroic characters in a kind of religious hall of fame. This assumption can block readers from seeing the ordinary, unworthy, and often dark and sinful nature of many biblical characters—as we have seen in our survey of Israel's history in chapter two. On the other hand, when readers encounter immoral or violent behavior among the biblically elect, they can become disillusioned or confused, assuming that the presence of unethical figures in Scripture signifies divine endorsement.

Of course there are also exemplary characters in Scripture, even amongst notorious sinners: Abraham's radical faith (Gen 12:4; 15:6), Hagar's humble obedience (Gen 16:9-15), David's uncensored confessions and psalms, Jesus' incarnation as God in the flesh, the Apostle Paul's invitation to imitate him (1 Cor 4:15).

Jesus and the apostles model frontal attacks against moralism and heroism. Jesus says to the scribes and Pharisees, "You say, 'If we had been living in the days of our fathers, we would not have been partners with them in shedding the blood of the prophets.' So you testify against yourselves, that you are sons of those who murdered the prophets" (Mt 23:30–31). Jesus pursues, embraces, and befriends the excluded and sinners, reinforcing God's consistent choice of the sinful and undeserving, including his own people, Israel. Paul has strong words of warning against the danger of coming under the law versus living by grace: "And I testify again to every man who receives circumcision, that he is under obligation to keep the whole Law. You have been severed from Christ, you who are seeking to be justified by law; you have fallen from grace" (Gal 5:4–5).

Further reflection: Can you commit to reading the Bible regularly for messages of hope for criminals, addicts, or others who recognize their failure, including yourself? What signs of good news do you find yourself gravitating towards? As you continually rediscover God's love for the undeserving in biblical texts, your confidence in the transformational power of God's Word will increase.

Passivity

Passivity is a reaction to legalism, moralism, or heroism that involves inaction based on a radical commitment to salvation by grace. Passivity can result when we embrace an image of Jesus as an inclusive, benevolent friend who offers total acceptance regardless of people's past behavior and future choices. While Jesus certainly embraces people regardless of their sin, he never leaves people in their broken state. He calls them to freedom, healing, and a new life of radical trust that involves following him day by day.

Passivity also results when we read the Bible with a deliberate refusal to respond for ideological or theological reasons. We can become trapped inside a passive mindset when we insist that grace requires nothing, which becomes a new "right" versus the "wrong" of acting in compliance with Scripture to please God. Jesus offers another alternative. He invites us to trust his living word and choose life rather than death. We stumble into this pitfall when we relate to an intellectual reconstruction of Jesus rather than risk relating to the living Christ. Following Jesus involves surrendering our control and stepping into a freedom that often feels precarious and looks messy.

Further reflection: Do you ever notice an emphasis on salvation by grace having a demobilizing effect on yourself or people around you? When and where to you see this?

Fatalism

A common belief system that contributes to passivity is fatalism, which assumes that everything that happens is part of God's sovereign, unchangeable blueprint. If God is viewed as a celestial sovereign who masterminds and controls all events, there's little to no room for humans to choose to exercise their authority. This viewpoint doesn't take into account human responsibility for evil, or recognize Satan as still functioning as the "ruler of this world." God is consequently blamed for everything negative, disempowering humans from active resistance to evil through active obedience to God's word discerned through prayer, dialogue with others and study of Scripture.

Unbelief and Cynicism

Unbelief and cynicism are pitfalls common in educated, Western circles, where everything is viewed with suspicion and subject to falsification. When we value mistrust as a virtue, we will find it difficult to build a relationship of trust in an invisible God, who reveals, in part, through Scripture, which was written by imperfect humans. Faith involves choosing to believe and trust, sometimes despite the evidence. This posture nurtures expectation within us, which helps us identify and receive the good news of God's love through Scripture. Sometimes we must deliberately renounce pride and fear to enter into a life of belief and trust.

Further reflection: What are some of the reasons you or others engage in unbelief or cynicism? Make a list of beliefs you think are required of you which you struggle with in your following of Jesus. Ask the Holy Spirit to highlight one or more questions you have. Ask God for clarity regarding your highlighted question. Try experimenting with faith by choosing to act upon any clarity you receive as if it were true. What do you notice as you do this?

Compulsion to Prove

The compulsion to prove any particular belief using the Bible is another pitfall that blocks fresh, life-giving interpretation. When we seek evidence in Scripture for a theological position, we might simplify or misread texts to make them fit our biases. We may pursue evidence in the Bible to support a message we find appealing or necessary. We may feel compelled to disprove theological positions that we consider destructive or annoying. Other times we may want to convince ourselves or others about a truth that we think needs to be emphasized. But this pressure often comes from fear and insecurity, and it can cause us to read particular texts out of context, missing deeper insights.

Further reflection: What are your motivations and filters as you read the Bible? What barriers do you face as you seek to be more open and trusting?

Need to Control

The need to be in control or succeed is related to the compulsion to prove. Naturally, we want to be right, to justify ourselves and our group, to have everything figured out, and to support our worldviews and lifestyle choices. But the need to control can actually reflect a desire to be independent from God. For when we choose to call the shots, we actively rebel against God. The fear of failure or of losing control is often rooted in pride and self-sufficiency. We may be tempted to trust in a system of thinking or ideology for our security and success rather than on a dynamic relationship with a living God. When we read the Bible or lead Bible studies from this foundation, we will inevitably resist the Spirit's mind-transforming action. Following Jesus as our rabbi involves continual surrender and deliberate trust, which will allow the Holy Spirit to lead us and continually transform our minds. As Paul writes in Romans 12:1–2:

> Therefore I urge you, brethren, by the mercies of God, to present your bodies a living and holy sacrifice, acceptable to God, which is your spiritual service of worship. And do not be conformed to this world, but be transformed by the renewing of your mind, so that you may prove what the will of God is, that which is good and acceptable and perfect.

THEOLOGICAL ASSUMPTIONS FOR LIBERATING READING OF SCRIPTURE

Many people happen upon the Bible and read it as they would any other book. Some people come to faith in Jesus by reading the Bible unassisted, prompting many groups to focus on making the Scriptures available to all.[7] Everyone approaches life (including Scripture reading) with beliefs that can be both known and easily articulated as well as hidden and unconscious. We claim to live our lives according to our ideal beliefs, but our deeper, core beliefs underlie our actual day-to-day decision-making. It is important to identify both our actual and ideal

7. The Gideons International is an organization dedicated to making complete Bibles and New Testaments available in strategic locations. See https://www2.gideons.org.

theological assumptions so that we can examine them and bring them into alignment with God's fullest revelation in Scripture.

In chapter two, we explored God's larger story of liberation throughout Scripture and highlighted Jesus' place within a Christian understanding of that story. We must clarify our theological assumptions in light of Jesus' earthly life, teaching, death, and resurrection, along with the apostolic witness, so that we do not misread either the Old Testament or the New Testament.

The Bible is an anthology of writings that tell the story of God's mission to save the world in collaboration with both the people of Israel and the church. The Old Testament recounts the story of God's establishment and accompaniment of Israel as God's chosen people over thousands of years. The New Testament continues the story of Israel with the story of Jesus and the beginning of the church. Christians believe that Jesus is God's son, Israel's Messiah, and the Savior of the world.

The Old Testament was originally written in Hebrew and Aramaic. In 300 and 200 BCE, it was translated into Greek, and is known as the Septuagint (LXX). New Testament writers spoke and wrote in Greek and therefore cited the Septuagint. Jews believe the Hebrew version of the Old Testament alone is the inspired word of God. Christians who embrace both the Hebrew Old Testament and Greek New Testament as inspired would do well to include the Septuagint Version since it is the Bible of the early church. Yet many assume their preferred translation is inspired "as is."

While it is always possible to read the Bible "as is," great confusion can be avoided when we approach it with some basic knowledge and keys to interpretation. Following are some core assumptions that I've found helpful in introducing first time readers to the Bible.

The Bible is human literature inspired by God

Scripture was written, edited and compiled by human beings from diverse cultures, time periods, geographic locations and languages. Biblical writers believed they were inspired by God to communicate spiritual truth to their communities. Later communities of Jews and Christians agreed on which writings mediated God's word. Jewish and Christian councils decided on their respective canons based on carefully discerned criteria. Since Scripture is human literature written in many distinct literary genres, it can and should be studied in its original language and contemporary translations using any and all approaches used for human literature. Since the Bible also mediates God's living Word, its meaning must also be discerned through prayer, contemplation and group discernment in communion with the saints past and present.

Scripture Draws Us into Relationship with God

Scripture does not replace God, but draws us into relationship with Jesus. Paul writes: "All Scripture is inspired by God and profitable for teaching, for reproof, for correction, for training in righteousness" (2 Tm 3:16). While this is true, Jesus clearly states: "You search the Scriptures because you think that in them you have eternal life; it is these that testify about me and you are unwilling to come to me so that you may have life" (Jn 5:39–40).

Scripture calls us to love and worship the Lord our God with all our heart, soul, mind, and strength (Dt 6:4–6), and Jesus calls us to love our neighbors as ourselves (Lk 10:27). When we read the Bible from this perspective of love, we are seeking to know, understand, and follow the one we love.

God is Gracious and Full of Compassion

The Bible tells the story of the One God who graciously and compassionately pursues human beings in the midst of their broken families, misfortune, and oppressive conditions. God reveals himself in the Old Testament using the unpronounceable name YHWH, which is rendered Lord in English (*Adonai* in Hebrew, *Kyrios* in Greek). The Lord becomes flesh and is most fully revealed in Jesus of Nazareth, God's son. Yet this Lord in both the Old Testament and the New Testament is the same God—Father, Son, and Holy Spirit. God desires and pursues relationship with people as a father would his children, extending special love for sinners—the violent, immoral, and excluded. The Lord chooses broken individuals and the nation of Israel—not as an endorsement of their characters or actions, but as a sign of God's abundant grace and love.

Jesus is the Revelation of God

Jesus is the most total revelation of the Old Testament God, Lord, and Father. Jesus is identified as Lord throughout the New Testament.[8] He is presented as "the image of the invisible God" (Col 1:15), "the radiance of His glory and the exact representation of His nature" (Heb 1:3), the one who reveals God the Father (Jn 1:18; 14:9–11), and who brings full clarity (Jn 1:18; Heb 1:3; Col 1:15). New Testament descriptions of the life and teaching of Jesus clarify misunderstandings that one might have about Old Testament depictions of God. Jesus reveals a God who comes to heal and not afflict, embrace and not reject, include and not exclude, forgive and not condemn.

Furthermore, Jesus interprets the Old Testament as bearing witness to himself as Israel's and the world's Messiah Savior. The New Testament presents Jesus as the anticipated Messiah (Christ) who is announced in the Torah and Prophets. The transfiguration identifies Jesus as the one to whom the Father calls people to listen, highlighting him above the Law (Moses) and the Prophets (Elijah). On the road to Emmaus, the resurrected Christ comes alongside his bewildered disciples, teaching them that the Old Testament, Law, and Prophets bear witness to a suffering Messiah.

Jesus Embodies God's Relentless Love

Jesus embodies God's relentless love and pursuit of sinners and God's compassion for the poor and oppressed. Jesus' very name comes with the prophecy: "he will save the people from their sins" (Mt 1:21). His opponents label him negatively as "a friend of sinners," (Mt 11:19; Lk 7:34), and many tax-collectors and sinners follow him (Mk 2:15). He is regularly judged for his close association with others who are viewed as sinners (Lk 7:39). "It is not those who are healthy who need a physician," Jesus says, "but those who are sick. I did not come to call the righteous, but sinners" (Mk 2:17; Mt 9:13). Jesus identifies himself with a shepherd who leaves the ninety-nine to seek after the lost sheep until he finds it (Lk 15:4), and he states that he has come "to seek and save that which was lost" (Lk 18:10). Finally, he receives the death penalty between two thieves (Lk 23:33).

8. See Acts 2:36 and others.

In Jesus, we see that God as Father, Son, and Holy Spirit is completely good. The burden of proof for God's goodness does not rest on God, but by faith we choose to trust that God is totally, unquestionably good, and we read the Bible with this in mind.

Scripture assumes a cosmic fall and predatory evil, and God enlists humans to resist

God's creating action happens amidst hostile powers governed by a third party enemy at war with God (Rev 12:9), referred to by Jesus as the "ruler of this world."[9] Human beings are created in God's image and likeness to "fill the earth and subdue it," and "rule over," resisting the powers of darkness (Eph 6:12).

Jesus Defeats the Power of Evil

Jesus defeats the power of evil on the cross, where the wisdom of God is revealed. This wisdom is "foolishness to those who are perishing, but to us who are being saved it is the power of God" (1 Cor 1:18).

Jesus inaugurates a new way of combating evil that differentiates enemies of flesh and blood from spiritual enemies. Jesus embodies active love of human enemies and aggressive combat against invisible spiritual enemies. Jesus' love of physical enemies triumphs over violent approaches that appear to be divinely sanctioned in the Old Testament. Jesus calls his disciples to follow him in this way of love.

Sin Does Not Separate Us from God

Sin does not prevent God from actively pursuing human beings. While we may rebel and turn away from God, our sin does not separate God from us. The common belief that sin separates us from God comes from problematic interpretations of several biblical texts. Jesus' words from the cross, "my God, my God, why have you forsaken me" (Mt 27:46), have been interpreted literally, suggesting that the Father separated himself from Jesus when he took the sins of the world upon himself. The argument is that since God the Father is too holy to look upon sin,

9. This entity is referred to elsewhere as the "adversary," the "accuser" (Rev 12:10), "the prince of the power of the air," Satan (Zec 3:1), the devil, the devil or the "Evil One" (Jn 17:15; 2 Thes 3:3; 1 Jn 5:19).

he had to turn away from his Son at the moment of his death, when Jesus bridged the gap between God and humanity. But Jesus is both the most total revelation of the Father (Jn 1:18, 14:7–11; Col 1:15; Heb 1:3) as well as the complete human embodiment of God (Jn 1:14). Thus Jesus' cry from the cross does not reflect God's abandonment of humanity, but rather God's total solidarity with sinful humans in the agony of death.

The belief that sin separates humans from God is also supported by a misreading of Isaiah 59:2: "But your iniquities have made a separation between you and your God, and your sins have hidden his face from you so that he does not hear." Yet the verse before this reads: "Behold, the Lord's hand is not so short that it cannot save; nor is his ear so dull that it cannot hear." Later in verse 16, the Lord is described as bringing salvation since there is no righteous human being on the scene. While humans may willfully run from the presence of God, God relentlessly pursues humans—and God's holiness does not prevent this.

Long before Jesus dies on the cross, God pursues sinful humans. God walks in the garden, calling, "where are you?" to the man and woman, who are hiding after eating from the forbidden tree (Gn 3:9). Once outside the garden God comes to Cain when he is angry and asks, "why are you angry?" (Gn 4:6). Throughout the Old Testament, God pursues Israel in her most sinful and rebellious states:

> I have spread out my hands all day long to a rebellious people, who walk in the way which is not good, following their own thoughts, a people who continually provoke me to my face (Is 65:1–2).

Jesus reflects God's closeness to sinners through the friendships he forms, the people he heals, the conversations he has—long before he takes their sins upon himself on the cross. God's closeness and continual availability to us when we need God the most is the best news that the world needs to hear.

Additional Pitfalls and Assumptions

There are additional pitfalls to liberating reading, along with many more theological assumptions, but I have focused on these because of their importance in the contexts where I have ministered.

Further Reflection: What are some of the operating assumptions that you can identify among the people with whom you read the Bible? What are some of the assumptions that you hold? How might these affect the way you interpret the Bible? Consider writing them out and prayerfully examining them in light of Scripture.

In the next chapter, we'll turn to a sweeping summary of the Old Testament Scriptures, with Jesus as our rabbi, discovering how Jesus embodies the fulfillment of Israel's sacred story. Then we'll journey alongside Jesus through the New Testament Scriptures and bear witness to the ways he continues to embody his Father's global liberation movement.

CHAPTER THREE

GOD'S GLOBAL LIBERATION MOVEMENT

Jesus of Nazareth embodied exemplary liberating action to advance the Kingdom of God in the world. His life and teachings in the Gospels both fulfill God's historic mission to save the world and set the bar for action now and until he returns. Jesus' life and our commitments to follow him today must be held within the larger history of salvation traced in the Old and New Testaments. Understanding God's overarching mission is essential for preparing and facilitating Bible studies that will be suited for our times.[10] In this chapter I will summarize God's mission and human responses in the Old and New Testaments[11] with the objective of clarifying some primary ways that God works in the

10. Summarizing the big story that Scriptures tell is a challenge. Within the Bible itself, there are many examples of summaries, which were all written to serve the interests of those who were writing the summaries. Abbreviated summaries in the Old Testament can be found in Ex 20:1–2; Dt 26:5–9, Jos 24:2–13, Jgs 2:1–3; 11:13–27; 1 Sm 12:8–12; Mi 6:1–5, Am 2:9–12; Neh 9:7–31; Ez 16–17, 20; Acts 7:2–53. Summaries of the mission of Jesus in the New Testament appear in Acts 3:13–26, 7:1–53, and 10:34–43. In chapter three, we will discuss how to summarize God's larger story in the context of leading Bible studies. For helpful summaries of the Bible's larger story, see Lesslie Newbigin, *A Walk through the Bible* (Louisville: John Knox Press, 1999).

11. I will focus more attention on the overall story covered by the whole of Scripture from Genesis to Revelation. In the Old Testament I will draw more heavily from narrative sections in Genesis, Exodus and Numbers, glossing over detailed descriptions of the law. Since my focus is to summarize highlights and overarching movements in the Bible, I will of necessity be glossing over vast sections of Old Testament prophetic literature and Writings, without even mentioning many important stories and entire books. My overview of the New Testament will also focus more on the larger narrative of Jesus' life and ministry and the beginnings of the Church, with minimal focus on the Pauline Epistles and almost no mention of the Book of Revelation.

world, avoiding pitfalls and keeping theological assumptions outlined in chapter two in mind.

The book of Genesis opens with a description of God on a mission in the world: God creates, the Spirit hovers, and God speaks into chaos and darkness. This darkness and chaos resembles post-war devastation preceding God's salvific creating in Genesis 1. By creating spiritual beings with free will, God opens the world to the possibility of rebellion.[12] Other biblical texts and the language used about beginnings suggest that this rebellion has already happened.[13] "In the beginning of God's creating of the heaven and earth,[14] the earth was formless and void, and darkness was over the face of the deep. And the Spirit of God was moving over the surface of the waters" (Gn 1:1–2). In Scripture, formlessness, void,[15] darkness,[16] and deep[17] all have strong associations with war, death, and chaos. Waters evoke the means of destruction of God's enemies.[18] God's Spirit is present in chaos and darkness, hovering over the waters, and God then speaks: "Let there be light, and there was light" (Gn 1:3).

God's words bring order, separating day from night, dry ground from waters, earth from heavens. God called the animals, birds, fish, and vegetation and human beings he created "good," and the completed

12. See Gregory A. Boyd, *God at War: The Bible and Spiritual Conflict* (Downers Grove: InterVarsity, 1997), 93–142.

13. See Is 14:12; Rv 12:9; Lk 10:18.

14. This is my own translation of Genesis 1:1, Reading the Hebrew *bereshit*, without a definite article, "in beginning of," and thus in alignment with Mark S. Smith, "When at first God created..." in *The Priestly Vision of Genesis 1,* (Minneapolis: Fortress Press, 2010), 44-45.

15. *Tohuvabohu* is associated with wasteland (Ps 107:40; Dt 32:10–12) and post-war devastation (Jer 4:23).

16. *Hoshek* (darkness) is associated with death (Jb 38:17), predatory animals (Ps 104:20), the absence of God (Ps 30:5), and threats to Israel (Ps 46:5). The removal of all darkness is associated with salvation (Is 60:19–20).

17. *Tehom* (deep) is the place from which judgment is released (Gen 7:11; 8:2; Ezek 26:19; 31:4, 15; Jon 2:5. The drying up of the deep is a metaphor for salvation (Isa 51:10). The Greek equivalent of *tehom* is *abyssos*, which in the New Testament is the place of judgment and death (Lk 8:31; Rom 10:7), the bottomless pit (Rev 9:1, 11; 7:10; 17:8) where Satan is cast (Rev 20:3).

18. *Mayim*, (waters) evoke the means of God's judgment (Gn 6:17, 7:6; Jon 2:5; Ps 124:4), the destruction of Pharaoh and his army (Ex 14:26–28, 15:8, 10), threats to life (Ps 69:1, 14–15, 144:7), and the destiny of the demonic powers (Ps 74:13).

whole "very good." God made people in God's image and likeness, male and female, and placed them over the entire non-human world, a concept that is unheard of in ancient times and is still revolutionary today. In ancient thought (and in many cultures still today), the material world was controlled by gods that needed to be appeased and bribed, and people had to submit to hierarchical structures.

Yet in this creation narrative, God gives humans, both male and female, authority, telling them: "Be fruitful and multiply, and fill the earth, and subdue it; and rule over the fish of the sea and over the birds of the sky and over every living thing that moves on the earth" (Gn 1:28). The creatures described as "every living thing" represent actual sentient beings, which in animist cultures— then and now— were worshipped in ways that reverse God's intended dominion. These creatures can also be symbolic of predatory evil, which pursues humans in a universe that is under the sway of the ruler of this world. God calls humans to multiply in the natural world for the purpose of expanding the kingdom of God.[19] They are to fill the earth, which belongs to God but is held under enemy occupation. By humans exercising their authority and engaging in spiritual warfare, God's reign advances.

God is differentiated from pagan gods through his personal name, YHWH (Lord). The Lord commissions the man and woman to serve and guard the creation, where predatory evil is already lurking. The Lord warns them of death should they eat from the tree of the knowledge of good and evil. But the man and woman are not vigilant and fall prey to temptation. They listen to the creature, a spokesperson for the Evil One, who depicts God negatively. Distrusting the Lord's goodness they believe lies instead. They step away from total trust, and fall prey to temptation. The Lord pursues them, showing them that their sin does not separate him from them. They hide, blame, and deny their sin. God banishes them

19. The Hebrew terms *parah* "be fruitful" and *raba* "multiply" are matched with *auxano* "increase" and *plethyno* "multiply" in the Greek Old Testament (Septuagint). In the New Testament *auxano* and *plethyno* never refer to human procreation. *Auxano* refers to the word of God (Acts 6:7; 12:24), the Gospel (1 Cor 3:6), and the knowledge of God (Col 1:6, 10) increasing. *Plethyno* refers to disciples (Acts 6:1, 7), the church (Acts 9:31) and kingdom resources (2 Cor 9:10) multiplying.

from the garden, which prefigures the Promised Land, understood as a state of grace and provision flowing out of a relationship of total trust.

Anger and violence increase, and the Lord characteristically draws close to the violent, banished offenders—Cain first, who is a kind of representative prototype. "Why are you angry Cain?" he asks, showing that sin doesn't separate him from Cain. The Lord pursues relationship, calling Cain and all who come after him to exercise authority against predatory evil, which is described as "sin crouching at the door" (Gn 4:6–7). Cain refuses to use his authority over anger and kills his brother. Murder, vengeance, accelerated violence, and the chaos of self-rule result, as described in the first eleven chapters of Genesis. God remains present to the descendants of the first humans, meting out restorative consequences, redeeming, and re-affirming the original mission to "be fruitful and multiply and fill the earth"—a pattern of things to come (Gn 9:1).

Human beings continue to rebel and suffer devastating consequences. But the Lord takes the initiative, calling Abram and Sarai from a life held back by idolatry, death, sterility and immobility. God makes a covenant with Abram and Sarai to bless them and establish them as a great nation. Through Abraham and Sarah and their descendants, the Lord raises up a people he calls to embody his liberation movement, through whom he promises to bless all the families of the earth. Abraham trusts God and becomes the founding father of different peoples and faiths, including God's chosen people, Israel. Abraham's son, Ishmael, who is born to Sarah's Egyptian slave, Hagar,[20] becomes the forefather of Arab tribes, and according to Muslims, to Mohammed. The Jewish people are launched through Isaac, whose son, Jacob, becomes the father of twelve sons, who eventually found the twelve tribes of Israel.

The writers of Scripture expose or "leak" classified information about Israel's patriarchs and matriarchs, political and religious leaders, and the people as a whole. The stories of Israel's patriarchs are surprisingly uncensored accounts of family dysfunction, including deception, favoritism, sibling rivalry, power-grabbing, polygamy, betrayal, incest, idolatry, rape, trafficking, prostitution, exploitation, vengeance, injustice, hunger, migration, and displacement. Every imaginable injustice and sin

20. See Gn 16.

is brought into the light in written form for all the world— past, present, and future—to see. It could easily appear that God has deliberately chosen the most broken and difficult individuals and family. Yet these narratives also depict the Lord as a merciful and faithful Father, pursuing, protecting, loving, correcting, blessing, guiding, and identifying himself with the unworthy. Some of the patriarchs and matriarchs pursue God in the midst of all the drama.

God continues to bless them by grace, increasing their herds and numbers, re-affirming his covenant with each successive generation. At the end of Genesis, Jacob and his twelve sons are all in Egypt, which begins a period of four hundred years of slavery.

GOD'S RELENTLESS PURSUIT

God's chosen people, Israel, multiply under Egyptian imperial domination, revealing God's faithfulness to his covenant promises and his care for the poor and oppressed. In the book of Exodus, we see how Pharaoh's genocidal campaigns against Israelite baby boys are resisted by numerous women characters, who disregard the law by protecting Moses. As a young man, Moses kills an Egyptian taskmaster and escapes as a fugitive. The Lord hears the cries of his people and responds by pursuing Moses in the desert, calling him to liberate his enslaved people, and then lead them to the Promised Land. God judges the oppressive Egyptian powers through signs, wonders, and plagues that provoke Pharaoh to release Israel into their destiny. But then Pharaoh and his armies pursue the fleeing slaves, only to be destroyed by the Lord in the Red Sea—a foretaste of the final destiny of the powers.

The Lord journeys with the people of Israel through the wilderness, encountering them at Mt. Sinai. There he gives them the Torah (law) with detailed life instructions intended to keep them free and set apart as a kingdom of priests.[21] Yet the people are prone to unbelief and rebellion, despite the Lord and Moses' best efforts. They repeatedly complain that they want to return to Egypt, then fall back into idolatry, and rebel. The Lord painstakingly pastors them through Moses and his leaders, disci-

21. See Ex 19:6.

plining, forgiving, and challenging them to put their total trust in him as their God.

Finally, at the end of the book of Numbers, Israel arrives at the land of Canaan, under the leadership of Moses' successor, Joshua, who leads them across the Jordan, into the Promised Land. In the books of Deuteronomy and Joshua, the Lord instructs the armies of Israel to drive out or destroy local inhabitants, who are depicted as antagonists, submerged in idolatry and committed to Israel's annihilation. Following God's precise commands to take the land from hostile powers, which vastly outnumbers them, this movement of liberated slaves functions like a guerrilla army, taking the land as a beachhead for God's global liberation movement.

Though Israel does take possession of the land, they repeatedly fall into temptation. They forget their history with the Lord, worship Canaanite gods,[22] and oppress their own poor. The book of Judges contains an oft-repeated description of Israel's relapsing:

> Then the sons of Israel did evil in the sight of the LORD and served the Baals, and they forsook the LORD, the God of their fathers, who had brought them out of the land of Egypt, and followed other gods from among the gods of the peoples who were around them, and bowed themselves down to them (2:11–12).

The people of Israel are repeatedly subjugated by predatory, dominating powers in the land of Canaan, and cry out to God for mercy over and over again.[23] God repeatedly shows mercy to the people of Israel, liberating them though inspired leaders, who are called judges. The people are serial offenders, repeatedly doing what is right in their own eyes,[24] turning away from the Lord in favor of idol worship, genocidal invasions, civil war, and myriad oppressive behaviors. The Lord is a serial savior, who relentlessly pursues his people and persistently seeks to save them. Even so, as we move into 1 Samuel we see that Israel eventually demands to be governed by a king, just like all the other nations, in spite of prophet Samuel's detailed warning of ruinous consequences (1 Sam 8:8-22).

22. See Jgs 3:7–8, 6:1–2, 10:6.

23. See Jgs 3:9, 6:7, 10:10.

24. Jgs 17:6, 21:25.

The Lord raises up prophets, through whom he works to select, anoint, and hold Israel's kings accountable by exposing injustice and confronting perpetrators. Yet Israelite kingship starts out disastrously with Saul, who models decision-making independent from God because of his fragile, tormented ego. He collapses Israelite religion under his own command by offering sacrifices and steps out from under prophetic oversight. He consults sorceresses and seeks to destroy his rival, David, who is joined by disaffected men that form a guerrilla movement. In 2 Samuel we see how David eventually wins over Saul and becomes Israel's greatest king.

Yet in spite of David's greatness as an exemplary guerrilla warrior, psalmist, and "a man after God's heart," the Scriptures expose his hidden sins before the world. We read uncensored accounts of David's polygamy, massacres of enemies, executions,[25] and adultery. The prophet Nathan brings a message from God to King David, exposing his adulterous affair with Bathsheba and his murder of her husband, Uriah. Yet David is still negligent, failing to protect his own daughter, Tamar, who is raped by his son Amnon (2 Sam 13:1-23). David is passive regarding his sons, who become rival heirs of the throne. His son Absalom kills Amnon and starts a civil war against David. Though Absalom is killed during this civil war, God promises that an eternal kingdom will come from David's descendant: "I will raise up your descendant after you, who will come forth from you, and I will establish his kingdom. He shall build a house for my name, and I will establish the throne of his kingdom forever."[26]

Solomon, the son of David and Bathsheba, becomes the next king, and 1 Kings offers a characteristically uncensored report of his positive and negative activities. Solomon builds a temple in Jerusalem and is known for his wisdom, wealth, and bringing Israel to its heights as a nation state. At the same time the Biblical narrative portray seemingly unbridled polygamy, alliances with pagan powers sealed by marriage, and straying from the Lord due to compromises with other religions.

25. 2 Sm 1:13–16, 4:12.

26. 2 Sm 7:12–13.

In spite of Solomon's failings, much of Scripture's wisdom literature[27] is attributed to him.

After Solomon's death, Israel is divided into two kingdoms, Judah and Israel. God sends prophets to anoint and then challenge king after king, calling them to love the Lord with all their hearts, observe the Torah, and care for the poor, immigrants, widows, and orphans. Isaiah, Jeremiah, and every other prophet expose both known and hidden sins and injustices and announce God's judgment.

Though a small minority of these kings do "what was right in the eyes of the Lord,"[28] 1-2 Kings and 1-2 Chronicles present most as turning away from the Lord by worshipping idols. One king after another leads the people to worship other gods at Canaanite high places.[29] They oppress the poor and persecute the prophets, whom God sends to warn and confront Israel. The Assyrian invaders carry Israel into exile. The Babylonian invaders destroy the temple and carry Judah into exile. Once again, God's people end up outside the Promised Land, where they began.

Even so, the Lord accompanies his people into exile, admonishing and comforting them through his prophets (Is 40:1-11). God affirms and expands his people's original call in the book of Isaiah, identifying them as the Lord's servant and tasking them to bring justice, teaching, light, sight, and freedom to the nations.[30] The Lord raises up a pagan leader, the Persian King Cyrus, to send the people back to rebuild the temple in Jerusalem,[31] which establishes the mission base in the land of Israel yet again.

The writers of the Old Testament daringly document their own people as a law-breaking, rebellious, violent group, functioning somewhat like a WikiLeaks for the people of God. Might these Biblical writers be delib-

27. By "Wisdom literature" I am referring to the traditional Jewish category known as the *Ketuvim*, including Psalms, Proverbs, Job, Song of Solomon, Ruth, Lamentations, Ecclesiastes, Esther, Daniel, Ezra-Nehemiah, and Chronicles.

28. See Asa (1 Kgs 15:11; 2 Chr 30:32), Jehoshaphat (1 Kgs 22:43), Jehu (2 Kgs 10:30), Jehoash (2 Kgs 12:2), Amaziah (2 Kgs 14:3), Azariah (2 Kgs 15:3), Jotham (2 Kgs 15:34), Hezekiah (2 Kgs 18:3), and Josiah (2 Kgs 22:2).

29. 1 Kgs 3:3–4, 11:7, 12:31–32, 13:2, 32–33, 14:23, 15:14, 22:43; 2 Kgs 12:3, 14:4, 15:4, 35, 16:4, 17:9, 11, 32, 18:4, 21:3, 5, 8–9, 13.

30. See Is 42:1–9, 49:1–6, 60:3.

31. Ezra and Nehemiah describe the rebuilding of the temple in Jerusalem.

erately presenting Israel as a sort of consummate violent and in every way sinful people group? If so, God's irrevocable covenant with the most notorious certainly offers hope for others who follow. The biblical writers' unprecedented transparency attests to the inspiration of Scripture—both because of their uncensored presentation as well as their revelation of a merciful and long-suffering God, who tirelessly and passionately seeks to save all who are lost. In story after story, Scripture reveals that no people, however sinful, are disqualified from God's pursuing, redeeming love. The story of the people of Israel might be read as a collective equivalent to the Apostle Paul's declaration in his first letter to Timothy:

> It is a trustworthy statement, deserving full acceptance, that Christ Jesus came into the world to save sinners [i.e., sinful people groups], among whom I [i.e., Israel] am foremost of all. Yet for this reason I[i.e., Israel] found mercy, so that in me [i.e., Israel] as the foremost, Jesus Christ might demonstrate His perfect patience as an example for those who would believe in Him for eternal life (1 Tm 1:15–16).

Israel never returns to its former glory. Rather, God's people survive under the cover of pagan empires: Persia, Greece, and eventually Rome. God's people appear as ex-convicts with serious criminal records and lifetimes of wreckage. Among this enslaved and oppressed people submerged in territory occupied by the Romans, God sends his son, Jesus, who is born as a descendant of David in Bethlehem, the hometown of the prophesied Messiah (Mi 5:2).

GOD'S RESCUE MISSION

Jesus enters human history to fulfill the global liberation movement initiated by his Father. He is revealed as the Father's only begotten son, embodying God's very presence in the world.[32] Jesus' mission begins with his baptism by John at the Jordan, the port of entry for Joshua's earlier entrance to the Promised Land.[33] Jesus submits to a baptism of repen-

32. See Jn 1:18; Heb 1:3; Col 1:15.

33. See Bob Ekblad, *A New Christian Manifesto: Pledging Allegiance to the Kingdom of God*, (Louisville: Westminster John Knox, 2008), 32–43.

tance for the forgiveness of sins, going under water in a symbolic death. In this act, he unites himself with the fate of the flood victims of Noah's time and Israel's earlier Egyptian oppressors, Pharaoh and his army, who drowned in the Red Sea. The Holy Spirit comes upon Jesus, and the Father identifies him as his son.

The Spirit then propels Jesus into the desert for forty days as a re-enactment of Israel's forty years of wandering in the wilderness. While in the desert, Jesus encounters the devil, yet holds his ground as God's Son against the ruler of this world by refusing to succumb to the devil's seductive strategies to sabotage God's mission of liberation for the whole world.

Jesus then re-enters the land of Israel as the new Adam and the new Joshua, inaugurating an unprecedented stage in God's original mission: to raise up his chosen people, Israel, as the vanguard of the global liberation movement to "fill the earth and subdue it" (Gen 1:28; 9:1), bless all the families of the earth (Gen 12:3) and bring reconciliation to all of creation (Mk 16:15; Rom 8:19-21). His people must first be freed from everything that demobilizes them. In alignment with Isaiah's declaration regarding the servant of the Lord, Jesus declares that he's come to preach good news to the poor, release the captives, restore sight to the blind, set free those who are oppressed, and proclaim the favorable year of the Lord.[34]

Jesus consistently distinguishes enemies of the flesh from invisible spiritual enemies, and he comes to "destroy the works of the devil" (1 Jn 3:8). Jesus begins his ministry in a Capernaum synagogue, driving out spiritual enemies (evil spirits) from one of his compatriots, healing the sick, and announcing the kingdom of God (Lk 4:31–36). He calls his people to love their human enemies while waging war on the invisible powers: casting out demons, healing the sick, and combating legalism. Jesus fulfills the legal prescriptions of the Torah in the light of the prophets, calling for compassion rather than sacrifice (Mt 9:13; 12:7) and inclusion of the unclean and unworthy rather than exclusion (Lk 19:10). This new movement will become the template for the future—a future that includes us.

At the margins of Israel in Galilee, Jesus recruits adherents for his mission. Over a three-year period, he trains twelve disciples to carry

34. See Is 61.

out the original and permanent mission of Israel's twelve tribes. He commissions them to go after the lost sheep of the house of Israel first,[35] demonstrating his Father's persistent pursuit of his people to become a missionary kingdom of priests for the world.

Jesus consistently focuses on seeking and saving that which is lost and emphasizes that no one is beyond redemption. He calls people to accept rather than exclude outcasts by healing, cleansing, restoring, and embracing lepers and other "untouchables" along paths, seashores, and mountainsides, as well as in boats, homes, synagogues, the Temple, villages, and cities. Jesus engages willingly and uncritically with women involved in prostitution, accused of adultery (Jn 8:1-11), or rendered unclean because of their ethnicity (Mk 7:26) or bleeding (Mk 5:29).[36] His actions demonstrate over and over again that sin and categories such as "unclean" do not separate people from the Father.

Throughout his life on earth, Jesus travels light, modeling a refusal to bow to the power of mammon or to anxieties about provision, clothing, or lodging. He invites his followers to "Seek first his kingdom and his righteousness," promising that "all these things will be added to you" (Mt 6:33). This path of trusting in God's kingdom ushers followers into economic freedom and relief from debt.[37]

Jesus' teachings and way of life enrage law-focused religious leaders, challenging their legalism and exclusive insider-outsider distinctions, while also exposing their hypocrisy and calling them into life-giving mission. The religious status quo is appalled by his close contact with sinners, his freedom regarding the law, the way he heals on the Sabbath, his bold forgiveness of people's sins, and his identification with God, whom he calls his Father. Threatened by his mass following, they appear jealous of his success and so plot to kill him.

Jesus was fully aware that his teaching and ministry would lead to increasing opposition and his eventual death. He warns his followers that

35. See Matthew 10:5–6.

36. Jesus' contagious holiness heals (and purifies) the woman with a blood flow when she touches him, rendering "clean" this one classified as "unclean" by the Mosaic law (Lev 15:19). Jesus cleanses lepers through direct touch and proclamation (Lk 5:13).

37. See Lk 4:19; Mt 6:12.

they, too, must anticipate struggles and persecution between his departure and his second coming: "They will deliver you to tribulation, and will kill you, and you will be hated by all nations because of my name" (Mt 24:9). He also warns of false prophets[38] and that some will come in his name, "saying, 'I am the Christ,' and will mislead many" (Mt 24:4, Mk 13:6). He describes a future with wars between nations, famines, and earthquakes (Mt 24:7), along with opposition from religious and governmental authorities (Mt 24:6–11; Mk 13:7–9). He says that his disciples can also expect betrayal and hatred amongst themselves (Mt 24:10). Before his death, he casts a vision of a future marked by apocalyptic turmoil, which will precede his return and final victory—when all will be held accountable and the reign of God will be established forever.[39]

Jesus equips his disciples for his departure by teaching them about his counter-cultural revolution, preparing them to minister in hostile territory and exhorting them to "be on your guard . . . for my sake, as a testimony" to those who persecute them (Mk 13:9). Jesus informs his disciples that "he must suffer many things and be rejected by the elders and the chief priests and the scribes, and be killed, and after three days rise again" (Mk 8:31). When Peter rebukes him for this prophecy, he rebukes Peter: "Get behind me Satan; for you are not setting your mind on God's interests, but man's" (Mk 8:33). Jesus continues to foretell his suffering, rejection, and death (Mk 9:30–32; 10:32–34), knowing that he is heading to the cross and the fulfillment of his mission.

Jesus warns that an increase in lawlessness will cause most people's love to grow cold, but that enduring to the end is necessary for their salvation (Mt 24:12–13). "Keep watching and praying," Jesus says to his disciples on the day of his arrest, "that you may not enter into temptation; the spirit is willing, but the flesh is weak" (Mt 26:41). In the face of growing global turmoil, Jesus keeps the highest priorities front and center: "This gospel of the kingdom shall be preached in the whole world as a testimony to all the nations, and then the end will come" (Mt 24:14).

On the night of his arrest, Jesus celebrates the Passover with his disciples. On Passover, Jews slaughter a lamb that symbolically takes the

38. See 1 Pt 4:1, 2 Thes 2:3; 1 Jn 2:18, 4:3; 2 Jn 7.

39. See Mt 24:29–30; Mk 13:24–27.

place of the firstborn son in remembrance of the eve of Israel's liberation from slavery in Egypt, when blood was applied over the doorposts and the lintel of the Hebrews' houses to protect their firstborn from being destroyed (Ex 12:7). Before Jesus' life is taken from him by Jewish religious authorities and the Romans, he freely gives his body and blood to his disciples in the bread and wine as God's firstborn Son. "Take, eat; this is my body," Jesus says, offering himself as the sacrificial Passover lamb, to redeem them from enemy control. He gives them a cup of wine, saying, "Drink from it, all of you; for this is my blood of the covenant, which is poured out for many for forgiveness of sins" (Mt 26:27–28). Without the shedding of blood, there is no forgiveness (Heb 9:22), and so in this way, Jesus fulfills Passover as the "lamb of God who takes away the sin of the world" (Jn 1:29).

In the New Testament the meaning and purpose of the death of Jesus is described in varied ways. "The Son of Man did not come to be served but to serve, and to give his life a ransom for many" (Mt 20:28). Jesus does not give his life as a ransom to those holding power, such as Satan or the Romans, in a way that legitimizes their power. Nor does Jesus give himself *to* God as a ransom in order to free offenders. Rather, Jesus mysteriously purchases people *for* God (Rev 5:9), giving himself in love directly to his disciples, who are called to receive him through active belief (Jn 3:16; 6:29) and participation in his life. "Truly, truly, I say to you, unless you eat the flesh of the Son of Man and drink His blood, you have no life in yourselves" (Jn 6:53).

God's giving of his Son and Jesus' active offering of his life to save humanity are an unprecedented, once and for all rescue mission. Jesus gives himself over as innocent victim to perpetrators who engage in committing the world's most monumental injustice and crime— the killing of God's Son, Israel's Messiah—the Savior of the world.

Israel's religious authorities, God's own people, plot his death (Mt 26:4), paying Jesus' disciple, Judas, to betray him (Mk 14:10–11) and sending a crowd to arrest him (Mt 26:47). The chief priests, the high priest, and the elders charge and condemn Jesus (Mt 26:59–66) and then mobilize the masses and Roman authorities to condemn him to death (Mt 27:20, 26). Roman soldiers dress him up as a king, mock and beat him, and then lead him to his death (Mt 27:27–31). Crucified between two criminals with a sign over his head that reads, "King of the Jews" (Mt 27:37), Jesus is enthroned even as he is rejected by his own people as the Messiah.

Since the wages of sin is death, Jesus suffers that death in order to overcome it for us all. As the only Righteous One, God himself, Jesus suffers and dies as innocent victim at the hands of religious and secular authorities — exposing the ultimate crime of Jewish and non-Jews alike for all the world to see (Jn 3:19). In this way Jesus both exposes human injustice and subverts the world's legal system. "Through death he renders powerless him who had the power of death, that is the devil" (Heb 2:14).

Jesus' declaration of forgiveness from the cross, "Father, forgive them for they know not what they do" (Lk 23:34), releases those who oppose him at the apex of their hostilities. Jesus preemptively forgives those guilty of the worst crime—killing God's Son, the Christ, Savior of the world. His forgiveness subverts any legal basis for a justice system that requires retribution. For at this moment, "God was in Christ reconciling the world to himself, not counting their trespasses against them" (2 Cor 5:19).

Jesus atones for the people's sin by offering himself up as a sacrifice to do away with the Levitical sacrificial system. God mysteriously makes "him who knew no sin to be sin on our behalf so that we might become the righteousness of God" (2 Cor 5:21), thereby demonstrating total love and grace towards humanity.

Jesus overcomes death when he rises from the dead. His resurrection strips death of its power as the ultimate sanction against lawbreaking and fulfils his Father's rescue mission to destroy the power of sin and death.

After his resurrection, Jesus appears to his disciples over forty days to declare his mission: "Go into all the world and preach the gospel to all creation" (Mk 16:15). The Gospel of Matthew records this mission in more detail:

> "Go therefore and make disciples of all the nations, baptizing them in the name of the Father and the Son and the Holy Spirit, teaching them to observe all that I commanded you; and lo, I am with you always, even to the end of the age" (Mt 28:18–20).

When the disciples ask if Jesus is going to restore the kingdom to Israel, he reaffirms the mission that will mark his followers until his return:

> "It is not for you to know times or epochs which the Father has fixed by His own authority; but you will receive power when the Holy Spirit has come upon you; and you shall be my witnesses both in Jerusalem, and in all Judea and Samaria, and even to the remotest part of the earth" (Acts 1:7–8).

UNLEASHING THE REVOLUTION

Fifty days after Jesus' resurrection, the Spirit is poured out on the day of Pentecost, effectively unleashing Jesus' revolution. The original apostles carry on the mission of Jesus in Israel, going out two by two as commanded by Jesus, experiencing both signs and wonders as well as the persecution he foretold.[40] New players join up, and the movement expands.

The Spirit of the resurrected Jesus appears to Saul of Tarsus, confronting him as he persecutes believers, and recruiting him as the Apostle to the Gentiles. Persecuted for his new faith, Paul writes important portions of the New Testament from prison cells. While under house arrest in Rome, Paul writes about God's larger plan to reach the Jewish people, interpreting his own Gentile mission as God's strategy to reach the Jewish people.

> But by their transgression salvation has come to the Gentiles, to make them jealous. Now if their transgression is riches for the world and their failure is riches for the Gentiles, how much more will their fulfillment be! But I am speaking to you who are Gentiles.... For if their rejection is the reconciliation of the world, what will their acceptance be but life from the dead? (Rom 11:11–15).

Other New Testament writers describe the eventual return of Jesus, the judgment of the world, the destruction of the powers,[41] and the coming

40. See Bob Ekblad, *The Beautiful Gate: Enter Jesus' Global Liberation Movement*, (Burlington: People's Seminary Press, 2017).

41. See 1 Cor 15:24–26; 2 Pt 3:7–13.

new heaven and the new earth.[42] Later, Jesus' disciple, Simon Peter, warns Christ followers that some will mock Jesus' second coming (2 Pt 3:3). The disciple James encourages Christ followers to remain patient and to strengthen one another's hearts until the coming of the Lord (Jas 5:7–8).

God's pursuit of Israel includes his non-Jewish church, which has been recruited to join God's global liberation movement. Empowered by the Holy Spirit, this liberation movement spreads to our present age. I invite you now to draw closer to Jesus and to consider joining him in this movement by embodying his kingdom and spreading it.

In the next chapter, we'll follow *Comandante Jésus* in his encounter with the Samaritan woman at the well in Sychar. This meeting and conversation will provide a valuable template to enhance your reading of Scripture—both on the margins and in the mainstream.

42. See 2 Pt 3:10–13.

CHAPTER FOUR

JESUS' RECRUITMENT BEHIND ENEMY LINES

Jesus embodies God's mission to save Israel and the whole world. The Gospels tell us how Jesus goes behind enemy lines, right into Roman-occupied Israel and into hostile communities and subcultures. There he preaches, teaches, heals, casts out demons, and recruits disciples. Jesus never leads an actual Bible study, but in this chapter we'll look at how he engages the Samaritan woman at the well personally through Scripture, her tradition, her community, and her own story, empowering her and calling her to new life (Jn 4:7–45). This contextually sensitive, transformational encounter is one example of what I'm calling a guerrilla gospel encounter or guerrilla Bible study.

John's detailed account of this empowering interaction provides a template for revolutionary encounters with God's Word on the margins, which we can apply to similar contexts today. Jesus' racial, ethnic, and gender profile establish him as a representative of the oppressive Jewish status-quo, which would traditionally exclude the Samaritan woman. Yet Jesus finesses this unequal relationship to bring good news to this excluded people.

CAMOUFLAGED GOD

John's Gospel introduces Jesus by talking about him as the Word (*logos*) of God, which is with God and is God. We learn that "all things came into being through him, and apart from him nothing came into being that has come into being" (Jn 1:3). The Word is powerful and inclusive: "the true light which, coming into the world, enlightens every person" (Jn 1:9). Yet at the same time, the Word is hidden: "he was in the world, and the world was made by him, and the world didn't know him," and his own people "did not receive him" (Jn 1:10–11). Although the Word "became flesh and dwelt among us, full of grace and truth" (Jn 1:18), he comes in under the radar.

This hidden way of God in Jesus encourages people on the margins, helping them feel better about the times they have failed to notice God's presence with them and also giving them new eyes to look for God differently.

Incursion into Samaria

Right before Jesus arrives in Samaria in John 4, we learn that the Pharisees are aware that he is baptizing more people than John the Baptist. The Pharisees don't like John the Baptist's renewal movement[43] and question him about his baptisms, but they are even more threatened by Jesus. John's Gospel emphasizes that Jesus' disciples are baptizing followers rather than Jesus himself (Jn 4:1–2), which indicates that Jesus' movement is spreading exponentially, since he is empowering disciples to multiply adherents faster than John. Twelve people are now baptizing rather than just one, multiplying John's impact twelve-fold. Jesus leaves Judea for Galilee (the remote backwaters of Israel) so that his movement can grow with less opposition from the authorities.

John's Gospel emphasizes that Jesus and his disciples "had to go through Samaria" (4:4). Devout Jews traveling on foot from Judea to Galilee could avoid Samaria by skirting the region, but this meant an additional three days of walking. There's no time constraint mentioned in the passage to explain why Jesus has to go through Samaria. The use of the Greek term *dei* (to have to) suggests that Jesus is compelled to travel through this forbidden territory.[44] Jesus expresses a similar compulsion using this term in Luke 4:43: "I must (*dei*) preach the kingdom of God to the other cities also, for I was sent for this purpose."

43. See Mt 21:25

44. For other references using this form of *dei,* see Mt 16:21, 26:54; Mk 13:10; Lk 12:11; Jn 3:7, 14, 30, 4:20, 24, 9:4, 10:16, 12:34, 20:9.

When Jesus feels compassion for the crowds who are "distressed and downcast like sheep without a shepherd" (Mt 9:36), he is similarly compelled to send out workers into the harvest, and he tells his disciples: "The harvest is plentiful, but the laborers are few. Therefore beg the Lord of the harvest to send out laborers into his harvest" (Mt 9:37–38, Lk 10:2). Samaria is in his sights as the place to extend his movement after Jerusalem and Judea (Acts 1:8). As the story unfolds we learn that the timing was ripe for Jesus to take the initiative in meeting this particular woman. This opportune encounter led to a two-day stay with a despised people group where many came to believe in Jesus.

Entering the Trauma Scene

Jesus stops at the outskirts of a town which is marked historically by trauma, injustice, and exclusion. Sychar, otherwise known as Shechem,[45] was in the heart of Samaria—a region inhabited by the despised Samaritans, who were religious and social outcasts in Israel, as they were considered inferior and unclean. Even the name Sychar might have been mocking slang, meaning "drunken town" (*shekar*) or "lying town" (*shaqar*).[46]

Much earlier in the biblical narrative, Israel's founding father, Abraham, passes through Sychar on his way to Egypt (Gn 12:6). Later, Jacob buys land, builds an altar, and settles in Sychar upon returning from twenty years of exile after fleeing his brother, Esau's, wrath for stealing his birthright (33:19). While in Sychar (*aka* Shechem), Jacob neglects to protect his only daughter, Dinah, who is raped by Shechem, the son of the leader of the city and its namesake (34:2). Two of Jacob's sons, Simeon and Levi, are enraged over their sister's defilement by an uncircumcised gentile.[47] (Sadly, they are more upset by Shechem's gentile status than

45. For strong support of Sychar being Shechem, see W.F. Albright, *The Archaeology of Palestine* (Harmondsworth: Penguin, 1949), 247ff. See also Raymond E. Brown, *The Gospel According to John (i–xii): Introduction, Translation, and Notes* (Garden City: Doubleday, 1966), 169 n. 5. See Leon Morris, *The Gospel According to John: The English Text with Introduction, Exposition and Notes* (Grand Rapids: Eerdmans, 1971), 257 n. 15.

46. See Leon Morris, *The Gospel According to John*, 257 n. 15.

47. In Gen 34:5, 13, the text emphasizes that Jacob hears that Shechem defiled Dinah, which outrages Simeon and Levi because defilement was synonymous with becoming unclean, through direct contact with the uncircumcised.

the rape itself.) They retaliate by convincing the men of Shechem to be circumcised as a condition for future co-mingling (vv. 7–24). Three days after the circumcision, while the men are still painfully incapacitated, Levi and Simeon attack the city, massacring all the men, taking their flocks, children, and women as booty (vv. 25–29). Subsequently, Jacob calls for a purge of idols from his family and moves them to Bethel, giving this land to Joseph's descendants (35:1–4).

During Joshua's leadership of the Hebrew people, the ancient Hivites of Shechem avoid death by concealing their identity as residents of the hill country of Lebanon and pretending to be worn out by their long sojourn from "a very far country because of the fame of the Lord your God. . . and all that He did in Egypt" (Jos 9:9). After the Hivites offer to be servants of the Israelites, Joshua makes a covenant of peace with them without asking for the counsel of the Lord (vv. 14–15). When the Hebrews learn that the Hivites have not come from afar, but have been living within their land, they honor their covenant of peace (vv. 16–21), possibly due to their ancestry to the circumcised Shechemites. But because of their trickery, Joshua curses them to be hewers of wood and drawers of water for the house of God (Jos 9:23).

Shechem later served as a city of refuge for people guilty of manslaughter (Josh 21:21; 1 Chr 6:67), but was also the sight of some of Israel's most horrific human rights abuses. Gideon's son Abimelech killed his 70 brothers in Shechem (Judg 9:5), before he was made king there (Judg 9:6). Later the people of Shechem set ambushes, robbing everyone who passed by the road. Gaal turned the people of Shechem against Abimelech, calling them to "serve the men of Hamor, the father of Shechem" (Judg 9:28). Abimelech retaliated by invading, burning alive 1000 men and women in the tower of Shechem and destroying the city (Judg 9:49). A certain woman[48] eventually killed Abimalech by throwing a millstone down from a tower he was attacking in the nearby village of Thebez (Judg 9:53).

Centuries later, the Samaritan woman in John 4 conveys no memory of Simeon's and Levi's misdeeds against the prior inhabitants of Shechem

48. The term used here in the Greek Old Testament, <u>gune</u>, is the same term used to refer to the Samaritan woman, inviting a possible rapprochement.

as she meets Jesus. Nor does she seem to remember Joshua's curse of the ancient Hivites of Shechem, nor the Israelites' scornful refusal of her people. Yet she is clearly wary about fraternizing with a Jewish man, which could evoke the land's historic memory of these troubling events. In place of a millstone, this woman carries a water pitcher.

SUBVERSIVE HUMILITY

As a Jewish man, Jesus is automatically viewed as guilty of holding negative attitudes towards Samaritans and oppressive male practices towards women. He also carries the destructive history of his people's actions against the inhabitants of Samaria. In a similar way, we carry the negative history of our own racial and national identity, and if we identify as Christian, we carry baggage related to our association with Christianity, Israel, the Bible, or our particular denomination or church. The Christian label encompasses the violence of the Crusades, exploitation and atrocities associated with colonialism and war, judgmental attitudes, legalism, collusion with the status quo, negative media attention, and myriad wounds that people have received from Christians. As long as broken human beings carry the good news, such negative associations with Christianity will remain inevitable.

And yet Jesus' identification with humans also means that God chooses to be mediated through each of us. In my story, this means that God can work through me despite my male gender, American nationality, Caucasian race, and every other negative or positive aspect of my personality. Though the details are different, the same question holds true for everyone: how do we acknowledge our identities when ministering among people who might be offended by our personal histories? In the rest of this chapter, we will learn from Jesus as he slips into hostile territory, approaching the Samaritan woman across the barriers of prejudice, exclusion, contempt, and violence.

Jesus stops at Jacob's well on the outskirts of Sychar, at a public well upon which locals depend. He arrives tired from his journey on foot from Jerusalem to Galilee. He sits down by the well in the heat of the day, arriving before the Samaritan woman comes to draw water. I imagine him deliberately staying behind alone while his disciples head into town—a far less intimidating presence without an entourage of twelve additional Jewish men.

Jesus' twelve disciples go into Sychar to purchase food, which contrasts with Jacob's sons attacking the city of Shechem unawares in order to kill every man,[49] and Abimelech's retaliatory assault. Yet they're not approaching the inhabitants of Samaria per Jesus' instructions to his followers: "without a money belt" and "eating and drinking what they give you" (Lk 10:4, 7).

The Greek word for "well" used here—*pege,* which means fountain, spring—is not the usual term. This word is used previously in the story of the angel of the Lord, who finds Hagar by a spring after she flees from Sarah, who mistreats Hagar because of Ishmael, her son with Abraham (LXX, Gn 16:7). This beautiful association identifies Jesus as the Lord, whom Ezekiel later describes as seeking after his endangered sheep (Ez 34:11).

The term used here for "well" also links Jesus with Abraham's servant, who seeks a wife for Isaac from among his kin in Mesopotamia by asking the young woman to give him and his camels a drink from a spring (*pege,* LXX).[50] Thus Rebecca, the mother of the Samaritan woman's beloved patriarch, Jacob, is chosen. In a similar way, Jesus deliberately includes this excluded Samaritan woman as his special choice, with a subtle suggestion that this story is a betrothal narrative, where Christ as groom can be interpreted as pursuing a wary and distinctly disqualified potential bride.

When the Samaritan woman arrives, Jesus initiates a conversation by stating jarringly, "Give me a drink" (Jn 4:7). As a male representative of the dominant Israelite citizenry, Jesus commands a certain respect, possessing a higher social status based on his gender alone. As a Jewish man, he is prohibited by religious norms from having any public contact

49. See Gn 34:25–26. The language here also connects to Jesus' later offer of "a well springing up to eternal life" (*pege,* LXX).

50. See Gn 24:13, 16, 29, 30, 42, 45.

with a woman or any contact with a Samaritan.[51] He breaks these two rules[52] by asking her for a drink, and yet he formulates his request as a command so that she will not have to speak with him. He approaches her as a road-weary guest in need, though they both know that he will be defiled by drinking any water she draws for him.[53] He asks for hospitality from the only possible host present, approaching her as a potential "person of peace" through whom he might reach the larger community. This posture mirrors his instructions to seventy of his followers in Luke 10: "If a person of peace is there, your peace will rest on him; but if not, it will return to you. Stay in that house, eating and drinking what they give you" (vv. 6–7, emphasis added).

SUBVERSIVE VULNERABILITY

As an itinerant missionary, Jesus comes in vulnerability and need, embodying his instructions to his twelve disciples in Luke 9: "Take nothing for your journey, neither a staff, nor a bag, nor bread, nor money; and do not even have two tunics apiece. Whatever house you enter, stay there until you leave that city" (vv. 3–4). Though Jesus enters the mission field of Samaria without food or water, he's in hostile territory, and so he keeps a respectful distance rather than approaching the Samaritans' homes and saying, "peace be to this house," as he instructs the seventy in Luke 10 (quoted above). Jesus seems to recognize the woman as a functional doorkeeper to her community, and so he engages with her from a position of functional inferiority.

51. Jews do not use *utensils* with Samaritans. This was built into a regulation in AD 65 or 66: "The daughters of the Samaritans are (deemed unclean as) menstruants from their cradle" (Mishnah, Nidd, 4:1), i.e. they are all regarded as ceremonially unclean. Danby summarizes the complicated situation as "(a) a Samaritan conveys uncleanness by what he lies, sits, or rides on, by his spittle (including the phlegm of his lungs, throat, or nose) and by his urine; and (b) the daughters of the Samaritans even from their cradles (convey uncleanness in like manner), as also do the Gentiles" (Danby, 803; see also SBK, I, 538–60).

52. Morris, *The Gospel According to John*, 259 n. 25.

53. The Greek verb *sygchraomai* signifies "to use with," evoking the rule that Jews do not use utensils with Samaritans (Morris, *The Gospel According to John*, 259 n. 25).

As a representative oppressor to the Samaritans, Jesus models how we might prompt people's hospitality in hostile situations. He asserts his vulnerability when he commands the woman to give him a handout— a posture that reflects guerrilla combatants. Counter-insurgency manuals used in Central America during the 1980s describe guerrilla combatants as "fish" and those who host them as the "sea." Oppressive governments often tried to eradicate the guerrilla movement by draining the "sea" through the destruction or relocation of villages. Jesus is proactive, even aggressive in his dependence upon local hospitality. Confident that the Kingdom of God is better than anything this Samaritan woman and her community have ever known, Jesus risks his dignity to bring peace into a story of entrenched division.

At first glance, Jesus' command seems rude—unlike the angel of the Lord, who calls Hagar by her name and asks her about her life.[54] In expressing his need for water, Jesus is not polite, nor does he emphasize his own agency, as Abraham's servant does with Rebecca when he says: "*Please let me drink* a little water from your jar" (Gn 24:17 emphasis added).[55] It may be that Jesus is deliberately provoking offense to expose the prejudice and underlying hostility in his potential hostess.

Jesus invites the Samaritan woman to show hospitality to an unwelcome stranger or enemy by serving him a drink, a scene that evokes his parable about God's judgment of all the Gentiles (*ethne*) in Matthew 25 (v. 32). In Jesus' parable, those who give a drink to the thirsty are blessed by his Father and inherit the kingdom (Mt 25:34-35). In the story of Abraham's servant's search for a bride for Isaac, the servant's proposed and realized sign that he'd found the right virgin was the maiden's offer: 'Drink, and I will water your camels also' (Gn 24:14). The Samaritan woman falls short in both cases.

Jesus comes to Sychar as Abraham and Jacob's descendant to bless the city whose inhabitants Jacob's sons once massacred and to fulfill God's original charge that Jacob would be a blessing to all the families of

54. See Gn 16:8. See also my commentary on this story in Bob Ekblad, *Reading the Bible with the Damned* (Louisville: Westminster John Knox, 2005), 71–75.

55. Though in the LXX it reads more directly: "Give me a little water to drink out of thy pitcher" (Πότισόν με μικρὸν ὕδωρ, [LXX, v. δός μοι πεῖν]).

the earth: "Your descendants will also be like the dust of the earth, and you will spread out to the west and to the east and to the north and to the south; and in you and in your descendants shall *all the families of the earth be blessed*" (Gn 28:14, emphasis added). Jesus seeks to break down the barriers of separation between himself and the Samaritan woman, who is the potential person of peace, thereby opening the way for the city of Sychar to receive him so that he might heal the historic division between Jews and Samaritans.[56] In this way, he further embodies his instructions to his followers in Luke 10: "Whatever city you enter and they receive you, eat what is set before you; and heal those in it who are sick, and say to them, 'The kingdom of God has come near to you'" (vv. 8–9).[57]

However, the Samaritan woman does not give him a drink of water. She doesn't provide the needed hospitality. She's wary of Jesus and keeps him at a distance, revealing that she's street-wise in dealing with outsiders, especially men. Maybe she's interpreting his forwardness as presumptuous, a sign that he's looking for other favors or wants to dominate her. Maybe she's cautious about serving a needy man, which could lead to a co-dependent relationship she's deliberately avoiding.

SUBVERSIVE PEACEMAKING

Instead of giving Jesus a drink, the woman questions him directly about the racial and gender barriers that separate them: "How is it that you, being a Jew, ask me for a drink since I am a Samaritan woman?" She calls Jesus on his illegal behavior concerning both Jewish-Samaritan and male-female communication, "for Jews have no dealings with Samaritans" (Jn 4:9).

The Samaritan woman expresses the reality of exclusion that had begun centuries before. During the rebuilding of the Temple in Jerusalem,

56. As a Jewish man who represents to Samaritans one who would normally consider himself pure and in every way superior.

57. The stakes are high, since the consequences for cities that reject Jesus' followers are devastating: "But whatever city you enter and they do not receive you, go out into its streets and say, 'Even the dust of your city which clings to our feet we wipe off *in protest* against you; yet be sure of this, that the kingdom of God has come near.' "I say to you, it will be more tolerable in that day for Sodom than for that city" (Lk 10:10–12).

the Samaritans offer to help the recently returned Israelite exiles rebuild the walls of Jerusalem because they are seeking the same God and have been sacrificing to Him since they came into the land (Ezr 4:2). Yet the Israelites refuse help from the Samaritans because of their alleged idolatry, scornfully telling them, "You have nothing in common with us in building a house to our God; but we ourselves will together build to the Lord God of Israel (v. 3).[58] She demands that he explain his intention before she participates in lawbreaking.[59]

Jesus does not respond directly to the woman's hostile question. He remains silent about the racial, ethnic, religious, and gender barriers between them. Though he does not deny that he's a Jewish man breaking the rules, he doesn't apologize. Nor does Jesus defend his Jewish heritage, drawing from Scriptures showing Jewish gender or cross-cultural sensitivity,[60] offering Israel's best face as an apologist for God's chosen people—which are also his people. While Jesus doesn't present himself as a sensitive man whom she should trust, he also doesn't shake the dust off his feet and give up on the woman or her community.

Instead, he practices a kind of enemy love in response to the Samaritan woman's refusal to give him (her enemy) a drink by offering her an opportunity to receive a gift from God. But she must ask for it. Jesus describes this gift in a way that makes it seem distant as well as irresistible. With total confidence in God's gift, his own identity, and his capacity to offer the woman new life, he says: "If you knew the gift of God, and who it is who says to you, 'Give me a drink,' you would have asked him, and he would have given you living water" (Jn 4:10).

58. See 2 Kgs 17:24–31.

59. "What's in it for you?" she's likely wondering.

60. Jesus could have highlighted Moses' defense of the seven daughters of priest of Midian at a well (Ex 2:16–17), his interfaith marriage (Ex 2:21–22), Boaz' embrace of Ruth (Ruth 3-4), David's collaboration with Philistines (1 Sam 27) or other such examples of Jewish male defense or embrace of difference.

SUBVERSIVE HOSPITALITY

With these words, Jesus invites the woman to shift her gaze to the gift of God—this special living water. He does not tell her to ask him for living water directly, which conveys sensitivity and respect. Instead, he honors her wariness and distrust by appealing to her taste and discernment, assuming that if she knew the value of God's gift—and Jesus' identity—she would be asking him for a drink.

Though Jesus is still thirsty, he suddenly abandons his need for water. Recognizing that the woman doesn't yet know about God's gift of living water or who Jesus is, he shifts roles from guest to host, risking more of himself and transgressing racial, ethnic, and gender roles even further. In spite of his Jewish baggage and outsider status within the Samaritan community, he invites the woman to trust him.

Jesus' words clearly spark the woman's interest, for she responds by addressing him respectfully for the first time as "Sir," using the Greek term *kurios,* which is also used to translate the divine name YHWH (Jn 4:11). Yet rather than focusing on God's gift of living water, she asks a practical question about how Jesus will draw this water: "You have nothing to draw with and the well is deep; where then do you get that living water" (v. 11)?

She also appears to take offense at the inference that he considers himself superior because he is able to offer this special water: "You are not greater than our father Jacob, are you, who gave us the well and drank of it himself," along with his children and livestock (v. 12)? She challenges. Because the woman is used to being excluded, she wants to know if Jesus is dishonoring her cultural heritage or her ancestor Jacob and his well. If he's suggesting that Jacob is inferior she won't engage with him any further.

By coming to the well and asking the woman to give him a drink of water, Jesus has already humbled himself and shown honor to the well and also to the woman. But Jesus does not placate her by elevating her culture or Jacob as a patriarch. He does not call him "our father" —though he is a common ancestor. While the woman appears to identify Jacob as a founding father hero, Jesus doesn't expose her idolatry—nor does he critique Jacob for his negligence regarding Dinah or for the senseless massacre of the Samaritans by Jacob's sons, Simeon and Levi. Instead, he focuses on water.

SUBVERSIVE FAITH

With an implicit gesture to Jacob's well, Jesus tells the woman frankly, "Everyone who drinks of this water will thirst again" (Jn 4:13). And how can she disagree? Then he unabashedly claims that the water he offers is superior to this precious water, upon which the life of her community depends: "but whoever drinks of the water that I will give them will never thirst; but the water that I will give him will become in him a well of water springing up to eternal life" (vv. 13–14). Jesus offers to give something that will meet a need that no human patriarch or physical substance can fill.

By making such a hugely intriguing and attractive claim, Jesus invites the woman to imagine a seeming impossibility within the everyday grind of her normal life.

Even more compellingly, Jesus doesn't assume that the woman wants or needs this water. Instead, he offers the promise to "*whoever* drinks of the water" (v. 14, emphasis mine). This re-affirms the living and perpetually flowing nature of this water and models a way of offering good news that gives the woman the freedom to express her desire for the water or to decline it. With the words, "whoever drinks of the water," Jesus also subtly invites the woman to think beyond her personal needs to those of the wider community. For Jesus' inclusive offer is open to all.

The woman cannot resist this offer, so she says to Jesus, "Sir, give me this water, so I will not be thirsty nor come all the way here to draw" (Jn 4:15). Then Jesus steps up his pastoral pursuit to another level. He could immediately offer his living water to the woman before him, meeting her stated desire not to "be thirsty" nor to "come all the way here to draw." But Jesus is looking for something more, and he is willing to risk everything to see truth descend into people's innermost beings (Ps 51:6). "Go, call your husband and come here," he tells the woman, revealing God's care for her entire life, including her intimate relationships as well as her larger community.

REVOLUTIONARY VISION

When Jesus tells the woman to return with her husband, he brings into the light the hidden truth of her life. For "The woman answered and said, 'I have no husband.'" Her selective admission that she has no husband reveals her vulnerability and the possibility of her availability to Jesus. Rather than expecting the best of the Samaritan woman's self-disclosure or letting the truth about her current domestic arrangement remain hidden, Jesus speaks a prophetic word:

> Jesus said to her, "You have correctly said, 'I have no husband'; for you have had five husbands, and the one whom you now have is not your husband; this you have said truly" (Jn 4:17–18).

Jesus affirms the truth in the woman's answer while at the same time revealing that his love is not naïve and his gift is not offered out of ignorance. By affirming a second time that she has spoken the truth, he clarifies that he is not judging her.

The woman neither confesses nor denies her history with men, but she concedes guardedly: "Sir, I perceive that you are a prophet" (Jn 4:19). Then she changes the subject: "Our fathers worshiped in this mountain, and you people say that in Jerusalem is the place where men ought to worship" (v. 20). Whether this is an honest question that she wants to resolve, or an attempt to distract Jesus from her personal affairs, she remains wary about trusting Jesus.

The Samaritan woman wants to know if Jesus is asking her to change her beliefs and leave her religion and community in order to receive this living water from him. Historically, when the men of Shechem accepted Simeon and Levi's proposal to be circumcised, adapting to the Jewish religious practice in order to enter into full communion with Israel, they were massacred while in recovery (Gn 34:15–31). So the woman raises an old question that has long divided Jews from Samaritans: whereas Samaritans believe the Temple is supposed to be on Mount Gerizim in Shechem, Jews believe it is supposed to be on Mount Zion in Jerusalem.

The debate comes from Scriptures in the Torah that show Moses and the children of Israel setting aside Mt. Gerizim as holy.[61]

Jesus responds by refusing to take sides: "Woman, believe me, an hour is coming when neither in this mountain, nor in Jerusalem, will you worship the Father. You worship what you do not know; we worship what we know, for salvation is from the Jews" (Jn 4:21–22). Jesus takes her beyond her narrow notions of allegiance to the tradition represented by her forefathers. Though he includes her as a worshipper of the Father, he names her ignorance and also affirms the unique role of the Jewish people in bringing salvation.

In this way, Jesus invites the Samaritan woman into an alternative path to God:

> "But an hour is coming, and now is, when the true worshipers will worship the Father in spirit and truth; for such people the Father seeks to be his worshipers. God is spirit, and those who worship him must worship in spirit and truth" (vv. 23–24).

This appealing new path to the Father involves both Jews and Samaritans worshipping "in spirit and in truth." With ongoing wariness and intelligence, the woman appeals to a higher authority, the Messiah himself, whom she and her people are awaiting: "The woman said to him, 'I know that Messiah is coming (he who is called Christ); when that one comes, he will declare all things to us'" (v. 25).

REVOLUTIONARY REVELATION

Unveiling his camouflaged identity, Jesus says: "I who speak to you am he" (Jn 4:26). The language Jesus uses here in Greek, *ego eimi,* reveals Jesus as the God who also reveals his name to Moses in the desert, saying, "tell them 'I am' (*ego eimi, LXX*) has sent me to you" (Ex 3:14).

The arrival of the disciples with provisions from town interrupts this sacred conversation—similar to when the jail guards suddenly pop open the doors and announce, "Time's up." The woman leaves her water jar and heads for town, where she tells the men: "Come, see a man who told me

61. See Dt 11:29; Jos 8:33.

all the things that I have done; this is not the Christ, is it?" (v. 29). The woman has clearly received something significant in her encounter with Jesus, and what impresses her most is that Jesus knows her.

So begins God's revolutionary movement in Samaria. For after hearing the woman speak of her encounter with Jesus, the townspeople "were going out of the city, and were coming to Him" (v. 30). Longing to be known and loved, the women's neighbors are also drawn to Jesus.

In Jesus, the Word made flesh, God becomes totally present—full of grace and truth—to this woman living at the margins of Israel and her Samaritan village. In this sacred encounter, Jesus gets "away with" a guerrilla Bible study. The objective of a guerrilla gospel encounter is that Jesus might reveal himself through the Bible, the facilitator, and the group. To join Jesus in fleshing out the Word in grace-filled encounters, we need to be guided by the Spirit and sensitive to the truth. Spirit and Word need to embrace as we read, discuss, and enact Scripture, announcing the nearness of God's Kingdom—on earth as in heaven. Jesus' encounter with the Samaritan woman beside a well is the *now* of the coming hour, where true worship is embodied in Spirit and truth.

REVOLUTIONARY HARVEST

When Jesus' disciples return from the village with food, they are first struck by the fact that Jesus has been speaking with a woman (v. 27). Next they urge him to eat (v. 31). Jesus, like the Samaritan woman, also appears to be satisfied after their encounter, for he tells his disciples: "'I have food to eat that you do not know about'" (v. 32). Focusing on the material realm, the disciples ask one another, "No one brought Him anything to eat, did he?" (v. 33).

Jesus responds by pointing his disciples towards his Father's larger vision: "My food is to do the will of him who sent me and to accomplish his work" (Jn 4:34). Accomplishing the Father's work involves reaping the harvest, gathering in the fruit for eternal life. Jesus identifies himself as a laborer in alignment with his Father's harvest work, which he describes in Luke 10: "the harvest is plentiful, but the laborers are few; therefore beseech the Lord of the harvest to send out laborers into his harvest"

(v. 2). In the Samaritan narrative, Jesus invites his disciples into a new way of seeing the Kingdom of God that goes beyond natural seeing:

> "Do you not say, 'There are yet four months, and then comes the harvest'? Behold, I say to you, lift up your eyes and look on the fields, that they are white for harvest. "Already he who reaps is receiving wages and is gathering fruit for life eternal; so that he who sows and he who reaps may rejoice together." "For in this case the saying is true, 'One sows and another reaps.' "I sent you to reap that for which you have not labored; others have labored and you have entered into their labor" (Jn 4:35–38).

The story ends by describing how many Samaritans believe in Jesus "because of the word of the woman who testified, 'he told me all the things that I have done'" (v. 4:39). The woman here is depicted as reaping, gathering food for eternal life—even though she hasn't labored for it. The white fields ready for harvest are the people of her community, who the disciples couldn't see were ready. The Samaritans themselves come to Jesus and ask him to stay with them for two days, and many more believe "because of his word" (v. 41). These new converts go beyond the woman's confession of Jesus as Messiah, proclaiming: "It is no longer because of what you said that we believe, for we have heard for ourselves and know that this One is indeed the Savior of the world" (v. 42). I imagine Jesus and the Samaritan woman rejoicing together.

Most likely, the Samaritan woman and her community did not experience a growing well of water gushing up to eternal life that day. While teaching a crowd at a public Jewish feast in Jerusalem, Jesus proclaims: "If anyone is thirsty let him come to me and drink" (Jn 7:37). The release of living water for the Samaritan believers, those who responded to Jesus' invitation at the feast in Jerusalem, and any future disciples will come after Jesus' glorification. For while speaking to the Jews at the feast in Jerusalem, Jesus promises:

> "He who believes in me, as the Scripture said, 'From his innermost being will flow rivers of living water.'" But this he spoke of the Spirit, whom those who believed in him were to receive; for the Spirit was not yet given, because Jesus was not yet glorified (Jn 7:38–39).

Believing in Jesus is the first step in a journey that leads disciples towards greater empowerment to engage in Jesus' mission. In Luke's Gospel, this empowerment is promised on the eve of Jesus' departure, when he says: "I am sending forth the promise of my Father upon you; but you are to stay in the city until you are clothed with power from on high" (Lk 24:49).

CULTIVATING REVOLUTIONARY ENCOUNTERS BEHIND ENEMY LINES

The narrative of Jesus meeting the Samaritan woman at the well provides a compelling template for revolutionary encounters at the margins. At the beginning of the story, Jesus deliberately enters a region of an excluded minority, and he stops to rest at a well—a public place that people have to visit every day. Then he approaches an outcast woman from the position of a guest in need, breaking myriad social and religious rules. How might we imitate Jesus in our own incursions into enemy territory? Where might we identify contemporary "outcasts' in our communities and world?

Jesus initiates a respectful conversation with the woman about their common patriarch, Jacob, whom the woman knows from her tradition. Next he offers the woman a gift—living water—which he promises will meet her deepest needs. Then he reveals himself as the Messiah—one who can be trusted to bring about God's promises. In this encounter, Jesus models sacred conversation, which is at the heart of effective, dialogical Bible study. While he doesn't open Scriptures in this story, he is the very embodiment of the Word made flesh—full of grace and truth.

Jesus also respects the woman's privacy by inviting her to *ask* for the gift of the water—if she wants to receive it. Offering the water without her asking for it could strike a wary recruit as presumptuous, exposing her as desperate or gullible. So Jesus offers the woman a protective cover, leaving her complete freedom to exercise her will as a free agent. In leading guerrilla Bible studies, we need to learn how to cultivate a sense of protective anonymity for those on the margins.

I'm deeply challenged when I think of myself in Jesus' place, with someone asking me (however indirectly) for "living water," or some equivalent. As disciples of Jesus, how might we engage people with confidence in the "living water" that we bear, trusting that it will satisfy far more than their physical needs? Jesus' bold confidence invites us to thirst for the gift of God's satisfying presence, which we trust will usher forth a wellspring of hope and assurance.

While the woman reflects on the outrageous nature of this living water, Jesus reveals information about her life that only God can know. Then he extends the promise of this gift to her community, mobilizing her as the first missionary among this despised people group. "They were asking him to stay with them, and he stayed there two days" (Jn 4:40), which is what the first disciples did when they first followed Jesus (Jn 1:39). They then said to the woman: "It is no longer because of what you said that we believe, for we have heard for ourselves and know that this one is indeed the Savior of the world" (4:42).

Before Jesus himself entered this village, he recruits his disciples (and all who follow him) to join him in this movement, which he describes as a harvest.[62] Jesus himself engages in this harvest, and he sends out laborers: "I sent you to reap that for which you have not labored; others have labored and you have entered into their labor" (Jn 4:38).

I will return to this story of the Samaritan woman at the well in chapter six, looking at examples from this story to demonstrate approaches to more carefully read biblical texts. But first let's look at how those who are drawn to join Jesus' movement today can hear his voice.

62. See Jn 4:35–38.

PART II:

FACILITATING GUERRILLA GOSPEL ENCOUNTERS

CHAPTER FIVE

ALIGNING OURSELVES WITH JESUS AND HIS VISION

Jesus sends us out as his scouts and emissaries to connect with people like the Samaritan woman and villagers and guide them to him. Since no one can come to Jesus unless the Father draws them (Jn 6:37, 44, 65), we must deliberately and continuously align ourselves with the Father's will (Jn 6:38). The Gospel of John makes it clear that God desires for all people to experience permanent liberation (eternal life): "And this is the will of him who sent me, that of all that he has given me I lose nothing, but raise it up on the last day." (Jn 6:39).

We are the mediators of this connection, for as Jesus insists, "Truly, truly, I say to you, the one who receives whomever I send receives me; and the one who receives me receives him who sent me" (Jn 13:20). Paul echoes this when he writes: "we are ambassadors for Christ, as though God were making an appeal through us" (2 Cor 5:20).

When we are closely connected with Jesus, we can effectively participate in Jesus' liberation movement. Since Jesus is the shot caller we must learn to recognize his instructions. Following Jesus requires our ongoing belief, love, and devotion. The Holy Spirit refreshes our connection with Jesus, and when we align ourselves with Jesus and his mission, our spiritual authority will increase. For as John writes in the beginning of his Gospel: "But as many as received him, to them he gave the *authority* to become children of God, even to those who believe in his name, who were born, not of blood nor of the will of the flesh nor of the will of man, but of God" (Jn 1:12--13, translation and emphasis mine).

We are dependent on the Holy Spirit and the inspired witness of Gospels to clarify our perception and draw us to Jesus. When we choose to open our hearts and welcome Jesus, we "receive" him. When we receive him and believe in his name, we are spiritually born of God and adopted into a new family. We become increasingly secure in our spiritual identity as God's children, growing in our authority and empowerment as we continue to receive and believe in Jesus.

Active belief in Jesus enables us to minister as he does. Before Jesus is betrayed by Judas, he tells his disciples, "Truly, truly, I say to you, he who believes in me, the works that I do, he will do also; and greater works than these he will do; because I go to the Father" (Jn 14:12). When we believe in Jesus and invite others into active faith, we recruit people for his liberation movement in order to reach the whole world.

As we engage in Jesus' ministry, we need to be aligned with his revolutionary mission by remaining closely connected with Jesus, watching and listening for his communications, so we can discern his direction. Jesus tells his followers: "If you love me you will keep my commandments . . . and the one who loves me will be loved by my Father, and I will love him and will disclose myself to that one" (Jn 14:15, 21).

As we love and respond to Jesus, we will bear fruit in the Kingdom of God, for he promises that "If you abide in me, and my words abide in you, ask whatever you wish, and it will be done for you" (Jn 15:7). When we live in harmony with Jesus, he will sustain us twenty-four–seven, offering us logistical support from heaven. Spiritual backup includes practical on-the-ground instructions about tactics, strategy, and precise revelation about people, their contexts, the message that will reach them, and signs and wonders that confirm the validity of the word we proclaim (Mk 16:20).[63]

Jesus promises to send his Spirit to all his disciples in order to "disclose to you what is to come" (Jn 16:13) and to "teach you all things, and bring to your remembrance all I have said to you" (Jn 14:26). So how do we tune into the Spirit's disclosures?

63. See also Acts 2:22, 43; 4:30; 5:12.

For my wife, Gracie, and I, our call to serve the poor came through a combination of reading Scripture, prayer, study, and physical seeing. We studied Spanish and traveled in Guatemala in 1980–1981, witnessing firsthand the poverty of the indigenous Mayan people, hearing their stories, and experiencing the terror of a civil war. We felt the need to study the history of the conflict in order to understand its root causes and discern possible solutions.[64] We were also compelled to continue reading the Bible in search of direction about how God was calling us to respond. We founded Tierra Nueva in 1982 in response to the widespread poverty we saw in Guatemala and among peasants in rural Honduras. Later, in 1994, we launched Tierra Nueva in the Skagit Valley of Washington State after being impacted by encounters with Mexican migrant farm workers and jail inmates. In all of these places, we pursued approaches to Bible study that sought to bring the daily struggles and larger social issues of the poor and excluded into direct rapport with Scripture with the objective of personal and social transformation. One of these approaches to Bible study is called "see, judge, act."

REVOLUTIONARY PROCEDURE: SEE, JUDGE, ACT

"See, judge, and act" is a structured approach to contextual Bible study that began in Latin America in the 1960s and has spread throughout the world, mostly in Roman Catholic communities.[65] "See," the first step in the threefold process, involves recognizing what is happening in the entirety of people's lived reality, followed by efforts to determine the root causes. Careful observation of what is happening in the biblical text is also part of this process, which includes spiritual seeing.

64. See Stephen C. Schlesinger and Stephen Kinzer, Bitter Fruit: The Untold Story of the American Coup in Guatemala (New York: Doubleday, 1982), Victoria Sanford, *Buried Secrets: Truth and Human Rights in Guatemala* (New York: Palgrave Macmillan, 2003), and Daniel Wilkinson, *Silence on the Mountain: Stories of Terror, Betrayal, and Forgetting in Guatemala* (Durham: Duke University Press, 2004).

65. This approach is attributed to Belgian Cardinal Joseph Cardijn (1882–1967), a priest who ministered to poor workers and founded the Young Christian Workers and also influenced the Second Vatican Council, which is visible in Pope John XXIII, *Mater et Magistra*, no. 236 (1961).

The "judge" phase of the process involves drawing from careful observation, critical thinking skills, and the tools of social analysis to determine the root economic, political, social, and historical factors that influence what has been identified in the seeing phase.[66] The "judging" phase involves bringing a particular "theme into dialogue with biblical and theological resources through Bible study."[67]

During the "judge" phase, contextual Bible study can be enriched by incorporating valuable perspectives from the social and behavioral sciences.[68] The disciplines of anthropology, sociology, and psychology can offer a critical understanding of culture, society, and human development that can help the facilitator more sensitively bridge the gap between the biblical text and the people.

"Act," the final phase, involves allowing the insights from the previous steps to inform transformative action. The idea is that after we have judged a reality, we can act to change that reality so that it is in alignment with God's reality. This involves asking what kind of action best flows from the contextual Bible study.

"See, judge, act" is a fairly simple methodology for reading the Bible for illumination and transformation for our lives and world. When people who are accustomed to being marginalized share what they see and discern, their agency and leadership is strengthened. When educated pastoral advocates assist lay readers of Scripture to go deeper in their theological reflection, more transformative action can result. Both the "see" and "judge" steps make room for greater attentiveness and critical analysis.

In settings where religious people are perceived as judgmental, and where right or moral action is deemed necessary for salvation, the "see, judge, act" methodology needs to be adjusted to avoid reinforcing negative theology. For example, when working with jail inmates who

66. Understanding the biblical story in its literary and historical contexts and bringing the world and the Bible together for mutual enlightenment are also core commitments of liberation theology.

67. Gerald West, "Matthew 20:1–15: An Ujamaa Centre Contextual Bible Study." http://ujamaa.ukzn.ac.za/Libraries/everything/matt20.sflb.ashx

68. See Joe Holland and Peter Henriot, S.J., *Social Analysis: Linking Faith and Justice* (Maryknoll: Orbis, 1983).

have regular court appearances before a judge and experience public shaming from critical political and religious leaders, God is often seen as a condemning judge. For these people, the verb "judge" is inherently toxic. I prefer using the terms "evaluate," "discern," or "assess." Since many inmates tend to see Christianity as an expression of personal or social morality, I prefer replacing the word "act" with the question, "How can we respond?"

In the following four sections, I will examine how this contextual model for reading the Bible (seeing, discerning, and responding) is revealed through the prophet Jeremiah in the Old Testament, the prophetic and preparatory work of John the Baptist in the Gospel of John, the life and ministry of Jesus in the New Testament, and the world of dreams throughout the biblical narrative.

Prophetic Seeing in the Old Testament

Throughout the Old Testament, prophets combine physical seeing with spiritual or visionary perception. In Jeremiah, the word of the Lord comes to Jeremiah in what is essentially his first "training exercise" and asks him a question: "What do you see, Jeremiah?" (1:11). Jeremiah answers in a way that shows he is actually looking at something physical: "I see a rod of an almond tree" (v. 11). God then affirms his seeing and interprets the vision, revealing the picture as a poetic wordplay between almond tree (*shaqed*) and watch over (*shaqad*). This example suggests that images and sounds may be intentionally linked to broaden meaning. Moreover, God also reveals the additional information needed to interpret the vision: "Then the Lord said to me, 'You have seen well, for I am watching over my word to perform it'" (vv. 12–13).

In God's second training exercise for the young prophet, the word of the Lord returns to Jeremiah says, "What do you see?" (v. 13). This time Jeremiah describes a vision of something that is not material: "I see a boiling pot, facing away from the north" (v. 13). God responds with an interpretation: "Then the Lord said to me, 'Out of the north the evil will break forth on all the inhabitants of the land'" (v. 14). Then God describes the destruction of Jerusalem by the Babylonians (vv. 15–16), which is an ongoing theme of Jeremiah's difficult message.

In these training exercises, God alerts the prophet by asking a question that invites observation. In both cases, the prophet sees—first through a physical vision and second through a vision on the screen of his imagination. Then God interprets these visions, providing additional revelation that completes Jeremiah's understanding.

This pattern alerts us to the importance of attentive watchfulness, offering a clue about how we can expect God to speak as we lead Bible studies. To give an example of the practice of attentive watching in a prison Bible study, I once looked over at a man and saw on the screen of my imagination a metal bar coming down on his head. Looking towards him, I asked, "has anyone been hit on top of the head with a metal bar?" I was surprised to see five men raised their hands! I suggested that since God had brought this to our attention, we should pray for healing from head trauma. I prayed for those needing healing for headaches, memory loss, and fear to receive healing in Jesus' name.

A few years later, I remembered this experience as I was teaching in a church in Siberia, Russia. I wondered if the story might have relevance there, too, since it had suddenly come to mind. So I asked if anyone had been hit on the head with a metal bar. Twelve to fifteen people raised their hands, and I invited them up for prayer. Later, I learned that a common weapon on the streets in Russia is a crowbar!

Preparing the Way for Divine Intelligence: John the Baptist

In the Gospel of John, John the Baptist publicly states that he is not the Christ, nor Elijah, nor the prophet—but rather "a voice of one crying in the wilderness, 'Make straight the way of the Lord,' as Isaiah the prophet said" (Jn 1:23). He understands his vocation as the fulfillment of Isaiah's prophetic word. Then he sees Jesus coming and identifies him: "Behold, the Lamb of God who takes away the sins of the world" (Jn 1:29). How was John able to identify Jesus?

When John the Baptist first sees Jesus, he uses the Greek verb *blepo* (Jn 1:29), which is used almost exclusively for physically seeing with the natural eye.[69] When John the Baptist says, "I have *seen* (or noticed) the

69. In the NT, the Greek word *blepo* means natural, physical seeing, as in Mt 14:30; 15:31; Mk 5:31; 8:23; 13:2; Lk 24:12. In John's Gospel, it is used seventeen times, clearly signifying natural sight (Jn 9:7, 15, 19, 25; 11:9; 13:22; 20:1, 5; 21:9, 20) and including deeper perception (Jn 9:39, 41).

Spirit descending like a dove out of heaven and remaining upon him" (Jn 1:32), he uses the verb *theaomai,* which means to notice the unusual.[70] John the Baptist then says that he was prepared in advance to recognize Jesus in these ways. "I did not recognize him, but he who sent me to baptize in water said to me, 'he upon whom you *see* the Spirit descending and remaining upon him, this is the one who baptizes in the Holy Spirit.' I myself have *seen,* and have testified that this is the Son of God" (Jn 1:33–34). This passage uses the Greek verb *horao,* which includes full-spectrum seeing, and prepares John to identify Jesus and to notice the Spirit descending and remaining upon him at his baptism. Thus John sees and identifies Christ by using visual perception (*blepo*),[71] spiritual perception (*theaomai*),[72] and his imagination (*horao*),[73]

John the Baptist is sent into the world to prepare the way of the Lord, but he cannot recognize Jesus on his own. He needs prophetic revelation to help him identify Jesus as the one who will baptize with the Holy Spirit. In the same way, if we want to grow in our awareness of God's communication strategies, we will need to learn to perceive God's revelation in this full-spectrum way, including physical seeing (*blepo*), noticing the unusual (*theaomai*), and *with our spirits and* imagination (*horao*).

Jesus' Prophetic Perception

When Jesus recruits his disciples, he models prophetic perception as he speaks about their destinies and reveals things that only God could know. Simon must feel deeply known when Jesus notices him (*theaomai*), calls him by name, and then changes his name: "You are Simon the son of John; you shall be called Cephas (which is translated Peter)" (Jn 1:42).

70. This verb *theaomai* means "to observe something with continuity and attention, often with the implication that what is observed is something unusual" (J. P. Louw and Eugene Nida, eds., "Theaomai," in *Greek-English Lexicon of the New Testament,* Accordance Bible Software, 24.14.), or "to behold, look upon, view attentively, contemplate." Joseph Henry Thayer, *Thayer's Greek-English Lexicon of the New Testament* (New York: Harper & Brothers, 1889), Accordance Bible Software, 2300. It can include noticing the spiritual dimension of something visible in the natural (see Jn 1:14, 32; 4:35; 1 Jn 4:14).

71. See Jn 4:29, 45, 48; 5:6; 6:14, 22, 24, 26, 30, 36; 8:57; 9:1, 37; 12:21, 40; 15:24; 19:35; 20:8, 20, 25, 27, 29.

72. See Jn 1:33, 39, 46, 50; 3:3, 11, 32; 6:46; 8:38; 11:40; 14:7, 9; 16:16, 17, 19, 22.

73. Jn 1:50 may fit into this category. Also see Jn 8:56.

When Jesus sees (*horao*) Nathaniel, he prophetically names something about his character: "Behold, an Israelite indeed, in whom there is no deceit" (Jn 1:47). These words resonate with Nathaniel, who asks Jesus how he knows him. "Before Philip called you, when you were under the fig tree, I saw (*horao*) you," Jesus responds (Jn 1:48), inciting Nathaniel's exuberant affirmation of faith: "Rabbi, you are the Son of God; you are the King of Israel" (Jn 1:49).

Rather than modeling a way of seeing that is informed by rigorous theology and exegesis or careful social analysis,[74] Jesus models a hermeneutics of relationship that is grounded in love of God and love of people and the world. Over and over again throughout John's Gospel, Jesus insists that what he teaches comes from his Father: "My teaching is not mine, but his who sent me. If any man is willing to do his will, he shall know of the teaching, whether it is of God, or whether I speak from myself" (Jn 7:16–17). Jesus invites his disciples into the intimate communion he shares with the Father by abiding in him: "The words that I say to you I do not speak on my own initiative, but the Father abiding in me does his works" (Jn 14:10).

Throughout the Gospels, Jesus lives in intimate communion with the Father, by the power of the Holy Spirit, and out of a personal engagement with Scripture. He often quotes from the Torah and the prophets, such as in his inaugural sermon in Nazareth when he draws from the oracles of the Old Testament and reveals how he fulfills these ancient promises (Lk 4:16–21). Jesus also directly challenges common assumptions about the Torah,[75] the Prophets,[76] and the writings,[77] offering fresh interpretations. He teaches with remarkable authority, and his engagement with people flows out of his intimate communion with his Father. He strongly critiques the teachers of the law for being fixated on laws and traditions

74. This is not to denigrate the importance of careful study of hermeneutics, biblical and historical theology, exegesis, and other theological disciplines, nor liberation theology's powerful emphasis on *concientizacion*, which is the process of coming to an awareness of the root causes of poverty and effective approaches to liberation in solidarity with the poor. Rather, I am interested here in reflecting more closely on what we can learn from the Gospels about what Jesus knew and how he came to know it.

75. See Mt 5:27–28, 31–48; Mk 7:14–23; 10:2–12.

76. See Mk 7:5–13; 14:27.

77. Mk 12:10–11, 35–37; 13:14.

(Mt 15:2; Mk 7:8, 9, 13) and for not hearing or seeing the living Word when he declares: "The Father who sent me, he has borne witness of me. You have neither heard his voice at any time, nor seen his form. And you do not have his word abiding in you, for you do not believe him whom he sent" (Jn 5:37).

Jesus embodies the coming together of social prophetic critique and supernatural ministry in the power of the Spirit. Jesus heals the sick and casts out demons. He also exposes local and national injustice and defends the poor and vulnerable, much like Isaiah, Jeremiah, Hosea, or Amos. He denounces the religious leaders of his day for lacking compassion towards sinners (Mt 9:13; 12:7), for caring more about strict adherence to religious traditions and laws than about the welfare of people (Mk 3:1–6; Mt 12:1–8), for seeking their own honor and position (Lk 11:43), for holding back education from the masses (Lk 11:52), and for depriving the elderly of their financial support (Mt 15:3–6). When Jesus sees the rich putting gifts into the temple treasury, he notices a poor widow giving two small copper coins, and he elevates her over the others for modeling exemplary generosity (Lk 21:1–4).

He exposes the sin of power centers such as Jerusalem and accuses the religious and political leaders of plotting to kill him just like their forefathers (Lk 11:47–51), who stoned the prophets (Mt 23:37; Lk 13:34). He looks around[78] at the Temple and then returns the next day to drive out the moneychangers and overturn the tables (Mk 11:11, 15–18, Mt 21:12–13; Jn 2:13–18). Upon seeing a fig tree with no fruit, Jesus curses it, and it withers, an action that prophetically critiques the Temple (Mt 21:19). Moreover, he announces the Temple's forthcoming destruction (Mt 24:1–2; Lk 19:41–44; Jn 2:19).

Jesus calls people to resist economic oppression (Mt 6:25–34) and denounces the worship of Mammon (Mt 6:24). He has no illusions about political power and openly criticizes those who perpetually seek power (Mt 20:25–26), arguing that there will always be nations in permanent conflict (Mt 24:7). Jesus also has no illusions about the world getting

78. Jesus looks around (*periblepō*), a verb that signifies deliberately taking stock of a situation before acting. It occurs only seven times in the NT, six times with Jesus as subject (Mk 3:5, 34; 5:32; 10:23; 11:11; Lk 6:10).

better through human progress, but has an open-eyed critique of world history, which he knows needs a divine Savior (Mt 24:13–14, 29–31).

In these diverse examples, Jesus combines physical seeing with spiritual seeing in ways that challenge the separation between educated awareness and spiritual revelation. Jesus touches on this holistic natural-spiritual seeing in the Gospel of John when he says: "Truly, truly, I say to you, the Son can do nothing of himself, unless it is something he sees (*blepo*) the Father doing; for whatever the Father does, these things the Son also does in like manner" (Jn 5:19).

As noted in the section above on John the Baptist, *blepo* always signifies natural seeing, which suggests that whatever Jesus sees the Father doing, he sees with his physical eyes as he views people and their needs. May Jesus' seeing what God is doing in the natural inspire our seeing, increasing our expectation and alertness!

So when Jesus sees fishermen (Mt 4:18, 21) and a tax-collector (Mt 9:9), he calls them as disciples. When he sees a paralytic at the sheep gate, he asks him if he wishes to get well before commanding him to take up his pallet and go home (Jn 5:6). When he sees Peter's feverish mother-in-law, he heals her (Mt 8:14–15). After Jesus looks at those who criticize him for healing on the Sabbath "with anger, grieved at their hardness of heart," he asks the man with the withered hand to stretch out his hand to be healed (Mk 3:5). When Jesus sees the faith of a paralytic's friends as they lower him through the roof, he forgives the paralytic's sins and heals him (Lk 5:18–20). As he sees Mary weeping over her dead brother, Lazarus, he is deeply moved and weeps (Jn 11:33–35)—and then raises Lazarus from the dead (vv. 39–44). Upon seeing a large crowd, he feels "compassion for them, because they were distressed and dispirited like sheep without a shepherd" (Mt 9:36). This compassion stirs him to his call for a massive recruitment of laborers for the harvest (Mt 9:37–38).

Jesus also exercises prophetic insight when he reveals people's motives and what they are thinking in their hearts (Mt 9:4; 12:25; Lk 6:8; 9:47). In his encounter with the Samaritan woman in John 4, Jesus reveals personal information about the Samaritan woman's past relationships, which makes the woman feel so deeply understood that she feels compelled to tell the villagers to come meet a man who tells her everything she's ever done (v. 29). Many subsequently come to believe because of her testimony (vv. 39–42).

How does Jesus discern how to respond when he sees someone? How can we step into Jesus' way of prophetic seeing and responding with such clarity and authority? How can we align ourselves with God's communication from the heavenly command center? How can we perceive what God is doing and saying as we lead Bible studies?

In the New Testament, Jesus' physical seeing[79] leads him to decisive action, which reflects his priorities and passion while also advancing the Kingdom of God. As we seek to teach, preach, and minister from Scripture as part of God's global liberation movement, we will also need to pay attention to what the Father is doing in our listening, observing, and responding.

Seeing in Dreams and Visions

Along with physical and imaginative visions, God also communicates missional strategies, tactical objectives, orienting directions, and warnings to us through dreams. Since heaven is not on one particular time zone and God communicates continuously, dreams get messages to God's people while they're sleeping—like a nighttime inbox. Maybe the Spirit knows how distracted we are during our waking hours and chooses to communicate at times when our minds are more open and our defenses are down.

In Genesis 15, "The word of the Lord came to Abram in a vision, saying" precise words of comfort and promises of protection (v. 1). Joseph's famous dream regarding his brothers bowing down to him initially incites their rage and launches their plot to sell him into slavery, but it also prepares him for his future role (Gn 37, 39). Joseph interprets Pharaoh's dream about the future of Egypt, which leads to his exaltation as prince of Egypt (Gn 41). Old Testament prophets see what God is saying to them (Dn 10:1–9; Zec 1:7–8) and also receive revelation through visions and dreams (Ez 1:1; 11:1; Dn 4:5).

Visions and dreams are also common in the New Testament. An angel appears to Joseph in a dream, telling him not to be afraid to marry

79. The Greek verb here, *horao,* seems to include both natural and spiritual seeing, a kind of seeing God's purposes.

his already pregnant fiancée, Mary, because the child within her was conceived by the Holy Spirit and is to be named Jesus, "for he will save his people from their sins" (Mt 1:20–21). Later, an angel appears to Joseph in a dream again, telling him to take the child and his mother and flee to Egypt to protect them from Herod's genocidal campaign (Mt 2:13). The angel appears a third time to tell Joseph it is safe for them to return to Israel because those seeking to kill Jesus are dead (Mt 2:20).

The Roman centurion, Cornelius, sees a daytime vision of an angel giving him precise directions to a home where Peter is staying. While Cornelius' messengers are en route the next day, Peter goes into a trance while praying, sees the heavens opened, and visions of "unclean" animals descending on a sheet with orders for him to kill and eat (Acts 10:9–16). The Spirit then tells him to receive three Gentile men who are looking for him, people he would normally not invite into his home due to their unclean status. He goes with them to Cornelius' house, where he preaches the gospel, and the Holy Spirit falls on all who hear the message and then they are baptized (Acts 10:44–48). There are many other examples throughout Scripture that show how both dreams and visions are common ways through which God reveals and speaks. Such revelations require interpretation, wisdom, guidance, and faith as we discern how to respond.

God continues to speak to us today through dreams and visions. Once we begin to notice and pay attention to our dreams and visions, our awareness of God's revelation will grow. It is helpful to keep a journal and pen near the bedside in order to record dreams while they're fresh, so that they don't evaporate with the rising sun like morning dew.

As we practice paying closer attention to what we are seeing and perceiving in these diverse ways our awareness will increase. Broadening our exposure to life through relationships with people who are different than ourselves, travel, language learning, conversations, study, and deliberate reflection will increase our knowledge and further expand our perception. Conversation with God through prayer will further attune us to notice the deeper agenda of the Spirit in our lives and surroundings. Chapter six will focus on how we can pursuing this deeper attuning through listening prayer.

CHAPTER SIX

REVOLUTIONARY HEARING: TUNING OUR EARS TO DIVINE INTELLIGENCE

When we tune into prophetic revelation and act on precise instructions, what we "see" and "hear" informs us as we collaborate with God's mission to draw people to himself. Hearing from God does not require monastic discipline or access to sanctuaries or sacred spaces. God's Spirit hovers amidst chaos and darkness. God speaks in the midst of temptation, battle, approaching us as "a very present help in trouble" (Ps 46:1).

Yet the commonly held assumption that sin separates people from God often holds people back from expecting divine help when it is most needed. This viewpoint is expressed on the streets, in jails, prisons, homeless shelters, and also in churches. Many people think that God can't or won't ever speak to them positively. If God is pursuing them, it's to punish them—not to love and bless them. Jail inmates commonly criticize themselves and others as hypocrites for attending our weekly gatherings, because they don't expect God to help them now that they're in trouble, since they didn't seek God by attending church, praying, or reading the Bible before their arrests. The dominant belief system is that sin separates people from God's presence, disqualifying them from God's pursuing love. This obstacle must be deliberately and constantly challenged.

The book of Proverbs offers a powerful antidote to street religion, providing hope for all of us. I often invite people to read and discuss Proverbs 8:1–3: "Does not wisdom call, and understanding lift up her voice? On top of the heights beside the way, where the paths meet, she takes her stand; beside the gates, at the opening to the city, at the entrance of the doors, she cries out."

Then I ask people to identify *where* wisdom speaks. Together, we identify some of the high places, streets, intersections, and entry points of our own city. What if God is speaking to us in all these places? What if we could tune in to wisdom from heaven anywhere, anytime?

Then we read Proverbs 9:1–3, which describes wisdom as building a house, preparing food, and sending out maidens to the heights of the city to invite people to gather. The inmates are amazed by the way God's wisdom takes the initiative and calls out in the streets, in public places, and not in the expected places, such as church.

Then we read Proverbs 8:4–5: "'To you, O men, I call, and my voice is to the sons of men. O naive ones, understand prudence; and, O fools, understand wisdom.'"

"To whom is wisdom calling?" I ask.

Someone says, "God's voice goes out to everyone."

"To the ignorant, to the fools," someone else says.

"And who are the ignorant and the fools today?" I ask.

"We are," one prisoner says—and nobody disagrees. The men are surprised that wisdom pursues the uneducated and the undignified, the so-called losers who are on the outside.

I talk about how people usually think that sin separates them from God, but here we see that God's wisdom is offered freely to the unworthy, the unqualified. I invite the men to be on the lookout for this wisdom and to expect God to speak to them. I encourage them to consider asking Jesus directly for wisdom and understanding.

I invite someone to read James 1:5: "But if any of you lacks wisdom, let him ask of God, who gives to all generously and without reproach, and it will be given to him."

When I ask the men if any of them feel they need wisdom for a difficult decision, a relationship, or anything, everyone nods. We go on to read about the need to ask with faith, "without any doubting," with hopeful expectation that God will answer. I invite them to focus on a situation that comes to mind where they need wisdom.

"Let's take a moment now to ask God to give us wisdom," I suggest, and we all take a moment to pray.

One October evening, as I drove down to Washington State Reformatory, thinking and praying in preparation for our bi-monthly Spanish worship service in Washington's largest prison, I reflected on Proverbs 8–9. As I headed down Interstate 5 towards the turnoff to Highway 2, I asked God for wisdom. "Here I am, Jesus, at an intersection. Give me a word, give me wisdom that would open up the men to your love."

Instantly, I had a picture of a tattooed heart on a bare chest over someone's heart. I asked Jesus for the meaning, and heard the words: "People see you as having a black heart, but I see you as having a good heart and as being a noble man."

I immediately began to doubt that this was coming from God, as I had never seen a heart tattoo on a man's chest.

I arrived at the prison, passed through security, and made my way past the yard and into the chapel. A group of fifteen or so Spanish-speaking inmates were ushered in by a guard. I led them in a study on Proverbs, which came together beautifully. At the end I decided to ask if anyone had a heart tattooed on his chest. I looked around the circle from man to man, but nobody acknowledged such a tattoo. Then a man on my left raised his hand. "I do," he said in Spanish.

I looked at him and repeated the Spanish translation of, "people see you as having a black heart, but I see you as having a good heart and as being a noble man." His head recoiled, and another man exclaimed: *"Esta es una palabra profetica!"* ("That's truly a prophetic word!"). Then the man pulled up his shirt to reveal a band of tattoos running across his chest and pointed to a black-inked heart right over his heart.

Two weeks later, I asked him what the word about his heart had meant to him. He told me he was from a notorious street gang in El Salvador, had a long history of violent, criminal behavior, and was viewed by people as having a black heart. He said, "Lately I have been really doubting that people or God will ever see me as having a changed heart, even after all my efforts to follow Jesus. That word really encouraged me, giving me hope that God sees my heart as good."

This man was the most vocal leader of our new prison faith community, one of three or four members of a Central American gang. In the two or three years following his release, I watched him deepen his study of the Bible and grow in leadership as a street pastor in training. He refers to this word about his heart as a decisive moment in his call.

REVOLUTIONARY TACTICS: TUNING INTO GOD'S COMMUNIQUÉS

So how can we tune in more clearly to hear God's wisdom and receive clear direction about how we might follow Jesus today? Jesus' example and teaching about prophetic seeing and hearing are rooted in a long tradition, which is visible throughout the Old Testament. We must recover and actively practice these ancient ways of seeing and hearing so that we can receive clear direction now.

In Habakkuk 2:1–2, we see the prophetic stance that helps us position ourselves to see and hear from God: "I will stand on my guard post and station myself on the rampart; and I will keep watch to see what he will speak to me, and how I may reply when I am reproved. Then the Lord answered me and said, 'Record the vision and inscribe it on tablets, that the one who reads it may run. For the vision is yet for the appointed time; it hastens toward the goal, and it will not fail. Though it tarries, wait for it; for it will certainly come, it will not delay.'"

Mark Virkler uses these verses to teach four helpful steps in hearing God's voice: 1) quiet yourself down; 2) look for vision, 3) tune into spontaneous flow; 4) write it down.[80] I will present a complimentary version of the first three steps, highlighting some key differences for hearing the voice of God while preparing and leading guerrilla Bible studies.

80. Mark and Patty Virkler, *Dialogue with God: Opening the Door to Two-Way Prayer*, (Gainsville: Bridge-Logos, 1986).

Quiet Yourself Before God

Habakkuk positions himself to watch like a guerrilla fighter on the lookout for enemy action. Attending to what we see and hear involves active vigilance like a guard at a guard post. Standing keeps us from sleeping. Stationing ourselves on a wall means that we are actively looking for something. The imagery of a guard post and rampart assumes an encroaching enemy. But Habakkuk is also awaiting a word from God. We watch to see if whatever is approaching is a friend or an enemy, a true word from God or a counterfeit distraction.

Nearly all contemplative prayer practitioners throughout history, along with contemporary practices such as centering prayer, stress the importance of quieting ourselves.[81] To quiet ourselves, we need to remember biblical imperatives, such as: "do not be anxious" (Mt 6:31, 34), "seek first his kingdom and his righteousness" (Mt 6:33), "do not fear" (Mt 10:31), "let no one deceive you" (1 Jn 3:7: Gal 6:7), "keep watching and praying, that you may not enter into temptation; the spirit is willing, but the flesh is weak" (Mt 26:41). We also need discernment to distinguish between what comes from God and what comes from ourselves or another source. Finally, we need to be aware of the adversary's strategy so we can effectively resist its power. Che Guevara's council regarding guerrilla warfare is applicable to spiritual warfare:

> At the outset, the essential task of the guerrilla fighter is to keep himself from being destroyed. Little by little it will be easier for the members of the guerrilla band or bands to adapt themselves to their form of life and to make flight and escape from the forces that are on the offensive an easy task, because it is performed daily. When this condition is reached, the guerrilla, having taken up inaccessible positions out of reach of the enemy, or having assembled forces that deter the enemy from attacking, ought to proceed to the gradual weakening of the enemy.[82]

81. Cynthia Bourgeault, *Centering Prayer and Inner Awakening* (Plymouth: Cowley, 2004) and *The Heart of Centering Prayer: Nondual Christianity in Theory and Practice* (Boulder: Shambhala, 2016); Basil Pennington, *Centering Prayer: Renewing an Ancient Christian Prayer Form* (New York: Doubleday, 1980).

82. Che Guevara, *Guerrilla Warfare, Guerrilla Tactics,* http://www3.uakron.edu/worldciv/pascher/che.html.

The adversary is often defined in Scripture according to its functions, such as Satan (the one who accuses), the tempter, the father of lies, the thief, or the destroyer. So we can expect and rebuff voices, thoughts, impressions, and images that accuse, tempt, deceive, steal, rob, or seek to kill and destroy the good. The early church fathers taught that believers can silence these voices by invoking the more powerful name of Jesus, which brings the enemy into submission. As Philippians 2:10–11 declares: "At the name of Jesus every knee should bow, of those who are in heaven, and on earth, and under the earth, and that every tongue should confess that Jesus Christ is Lord, to the glory of God the Father."

Ask Questions and Voice Complaints

The prophet Habakkuk approaches God with a particular question and complaint—and then looks to God for answers. When reading Scripture with people, it is important to place their lives and heartfelt questions before God and the Scriptures, expecting God to respond. We see this in Habakkuk 1:2:

"O Lord, how long shall I cry for help, and you will not listen? Or cry to you 'Violence!' and you will not save? Why do you make me see wrong-doing and look at trouble? Destruction and violence are before me; strife and contention arise. So the law becomes slack and justice never prevails. The wicked surround the righteous—therefore judgment comes forth perverted."

Throughout the Gospels, we see the disciples, Pharisees, teachers of the law, and many other characters coming to Jesus with particular questions and needs. Jesus responds to each through words and actions: teaching, correcting, rebuking, healing, casting out, weeping, and sometimes remaining silent.

Look for Vision

Habakkuk stations himself to "keep watch *to see* what he will speak to me," which reinforces what we've already seen about how God speaks through visual images. The "see, judge, act" approach for contextual Bible reading discussed in the previous chapter emphasizes the importance of people carefully observing and analyzing both Scripture and their lives and contexts.[83] Observing societal injustice is essential to prophetic seeing, along with charismatic and contemplative approaches to spiritual seeing through the imagination, visions, and dreams.

In *Miracle Work: A Down-To-Earth Guide to Supernatural Ministries,* Jordan Seng offers the following insights about visions:

> When people ask me what it's like to get a vision, I tell them to try to remember the face of a childhood playmate. Most of my visions are like that—like having an image in my mind of something I used to see. The image may not be crisp, but I know what it is, and there's often an emotional or narrative sense about it—as if it has a tiny bit of story attached to it. So, it's both subtle and rich. I could easily overlook it, but having noticed it, I realize there's quite a bit to it.[84]

In Scripture, natural seeing is a catalyst for action that aligns with God's will. For example, Moses' mother disobeys Pharaoh's orders to throw her male baby into the Nile because she sees[85] that baby Moses is beautiful and hides him for three months (Ex 2:2). Then she places him in a basket in the river (v. 3), and Pharaoh's daughter sees the basket and calls for her servants to bring it to her (v. 5). When she sees the baby and recognizes him as a Hebrew, she has pity on him and adopts him (vv. 6, 9).

When Moses comes of age, he goes out to see his people. He sees an Egyptian beating a Hebrew slave and reacts by killing the Egyptian and hiding his body in the sand (2:11–12). Then Moses flees and becomes a shepherd in the desert, where the angel of the Lord appears (literally, "was seen") to Moses in a burning bush (3:2). Moses turns aside to see, a natural gesture of curiosity, and then the angel of the Lord speaks to him and reveals himself as the God of his ancestors (vv. 3–6). Moses hides his face in fear, assuming he is under arrest and on his way back to Egypt to pay for his crimes, but God reveals himself to Moses as one who sees,

83. See Gerald West, *Manual for Contextual Bible Study,* www.umjama.ak.

84. Jordan Seng, *Miracle Work: A Down-To-Earth Guide to Supernatural Ministries* (Downers Grove: IVP Books, 2013), 141.

85. In the Greek version of the OT, the Septuagint, *horao* matches the Hebrew verb *raah* in Ex 1–3 (see Ex 2:2, 5, 11, 12, 13; 3:2–4, 7, 9)—important backdrop for New Testament usage as we will see later.

hears, and knows the people's suffering, saying: "I have surely seen the affliction of my people who are in Egypt, and have given heed to their cry because of their taskmasters, for I know their sufferings" (v. 7).

The translation, "I have surely seen," reflects the doubling of the Hebrew verb *raah,* which evokes Moses' twice seeing in Exodus 2:11–12. This earlier seeing of the brutal injustice of an Egyptian taskmaster beating an Israelite slave leads Moses to kill the Egyptian. Now, God acknowledges Moses' first seeing without condemning him. Rather, he calls him into a deeper solidarity, which includes listening to his people's cries and knowing firsthand their sufferings. He informs Moses of his plan to liberate the people "from the power of the Egyptians, and to bring them up" from that place of slavery "to a good and spacious land, to a land flowing with milk and honey" (3:8).

God repeats that he hears and sees the people's oppression under the Egyptians, which reinforces the natural seeing of real injustice as God's very own prophetic stance: "Now, behold, the cry of the sons of Israel has come to me; furthermore, I have seen the oppression with which the Egyptians are oppressing them" (3:9). The Lord responds by calling Moses to liberate his enslaved people: "Therefore, come now, and I will send you to Pharaoh, so that you may bring my people, the sons of Israel, out of Egypt" (3:10).

Tune into Spontaneous Flow

God also communicates to us when we're awake through thoughts and words. These messages are more like voice messages than text messages, since we "hear" or perceive them rather than read them. In Habakkuk 2, the prophet states that he stations himself on the wall "to see what the Lord *will speak* to me." The Hebrew word *dabar,* which means "to speak," is used extensively throughout the Hebrew Bible when the Lord is speaking. The Lord speaks to Abram (Gn 12:4; 15:1,4; 17:22, 23; 18:33; 22:16), to Hagar (Gn 16:13), Jacob (Gn 35:13), and to Moses "mouth to mouth" (Nm 12:8). God speaks to his prophets—to Isaiah (Is 8:5; 38:4), Jeremiah (Jer 1:2, 4, 11, 13; 2:1; 7:1), and many others. The Lord also speaks to others through these people who hear and respond to his voice (Is 51:6; Jer 1:9). If we want our relationship to develop with God, we need to pay attention to his words to us: "'Hear my voice, and I will be your God, and you will be my people; and you will walk in all the way which I command you, that it may be well with you'" (Jer 7:23, my translation).

God's word is described as coming to people (Jer 11:1; 13:8; 16:1; 18:1; 21:1; 24:4). How might we identify and welcome these words? How can we know whether or not they are coming from God?

All of us have thoughts that come into our heads that get our attention. Sometimes these thoughts are negative and come as accusations, worries, resentments, and temptations. Other times commitments come to mind that we have on our calendars. We remember tasks or errands and reflect naturally on all kinds of things—relationships, work, world events, and so on. Words from God can also come into our consciousness in the midst of daily life in the form of reminders or reflections. Following are some ways that God seems to communicate with me. In every case, I test these words or impressions, almost experimenting with them empirically, to see if they are divinely inspired.

Thoughts often come into my mind spontaneously, without any planning or control on my part—much like when I have a dream. I wonder if this is what Jesus describes when he says: "I do nothing on my own initiative [literally "from myself"], but speak these things as the Father taught me" (Jn 8:28). Jordan Seng describes these spontaneous impressions as follows:

> A prophecy doesn't have to be a visual image, or course. It can be a word or phrase that emerges in your mind, or just some sudden knowledge or conviction that comes from nowhere but seems alive—as if you'd arrived at a conclusion but can't trace how. That is, a prophecy can seem an awful lot like what you might call a special thought. It has some heft, but it's in no way overwhelming. And the trick will be to notice it and identify its purpose.[86]

These spontaneous thoughts or impressions may come as a new idea that brings clarity to a question I have, a lead I can follow, or a question that opens discussion. If these leads are from God, they usually take me somewhere positive. When preparing or leading a Bible study, I often

86. Seng, *Miracle Work*, 141–142.

have questions about the meaning or application of the Scripture I am reading alone or with a group. Ideas come to mind that answer my or other people's questions or take me and the group in a new direction that I hadn't previously considered. It is important to consider ideas, questions, and impressions in a deliberate way, evaluating them before deciding a course of action.

Write it Down

The Lord tells the prophet Habakkuk, "Record the vision and inscribe it on tablets, that the one who reads it may run. For the vision is yet for the appointed time; it hastens towards the goal and it will not fail. Though it tarries, wait for it; for it will certainly come, it will not delay" (Hab 2:2–3). However, when teaching, preaching, or leading a Bible study, you might receive a revelation, and it may be important for you to speak out and act on it then and there rather than writing it down and pondering it later. But the Habakkuk passage does suggest that we deliberately reflect on prophetic revelation, which includes evaluating the word's veracity and timing. Scripture attests to the value of writing down God's words to individuals, communities, and nations. I suggest keeping a journal where you can record your thoughts, prophetic impressions, and questions. Writing things down invites deeper scrutiny and spiritual discernment.

I suggest running spontaneous impressions through a quick test, using the following discernment stool metaphor developed by Brad Jersak. The first leg of the three-legged discernment stool is *word*. Does the impression line up with the message and trajectory of Scripture? The second leg of the stool is *body*. Is the word given by someone in fellowship and accountable to the church, in alignment with the witness of the historic church, the creeds, and so on? The third leg of the stool is *Spirit*. Is there an inner witness of the Spirit along with the fruit of the Spirit when we act on the word? Jersak labels the seat of the stool "abiding."[87]

In reflecting on the seat of the stool, Jersak says:

> Anyone can get a Bible verse, a "yes-man' and a warm fuzzy feeling they think is the Spirit. What makes the stool more reliable is

87. Brad Jersak, *Can You Hear Me? Tuning In to the God Who Speaks* (Abbotsford: Fresh Wind Press, 2003), 87–96.

> the seat of abiding: abiding in the Word (saturating in Scripture until it oozes), abiding in the Body (with mentors and co-laborers who love you enough to say 'No, that's not God'), abiding in the Spirit (a regular practice of contemplative prayer so that conversation with God is in intimate friendship rather than intermittent 9-1-1 calls).[88]

Jersak has added a Christ-centered three-legged stool to his discernment toolbox for communities that may misappropriate the Old Testament. The first leg is the teaching of Christ (e.g., the Sermon on the Mount, the parables, etc.). The second leg is the character of Christ, as expressed in the Beatitudes and his interactions with others. The third leg is the cruciform life of Christ, which includes his Kingdom works and especially his revelation of God as self-giving and radically forgiving, as well as his co-suffering love expressed through the cross and resurrection.[89] These helpful criteria can help us evaluate the prophetic impressions, viewpoints, or teachings we encounter.

Once I've determined that an impression is in alignment with Scripture or the other criteria described above, I humbly speak out what I'm receiving. Rather than preceding a word with an overconfident, "thus says the Lord," I suggest a more tentative, "I'm wondering whether...," or "I'm getting an impression that...," or "Is this the case of anyone?" [90] This helps me discern whether potentially prophetic revelations are leading to greater clarity or understanding. If my impressions don't point in a positive direction, I abandon the thought.

Jesus describes his own actions and words as emerging outside of himself. One clue that helps me identify "things as the Father taught me" is that they don't come "from myself," but outside my normal thinking, such as interruptions or interjections. Jesus says that he speaks in alignment with his Father:

88. Brad Jersak, personal email to Bob Ekblad, July 25, 2017.

89. Brad Jersak, unpublished pamphlet, residential teaching seminar, Westminster Theological Centre (Telford, UK, September 2016).

90. See John Bevere, *Thus Saith the Lord: How to know when God is speaking to you through another* (Lake Mary: Creation House, 1999).

"For I did not speak on my own initiative [literally "from myself"], but the Father himself who sent me has given me commandment, what to say, and what to speak" (Jn 12:49).

Sometimes I feel compelled to interject an idea, ask a question, or invite response. These directives have some drive behind them and feel hard to resist—though, of course, we can.

When I was in the midst of teaching a group of 150 or so pastors and leaders in Tanzania, a strange question suddenly came to mind: "Are there people here who worship trees?" I continued with my teaching but the question persisted. Finally I stopped and asked the people: "By any chance is the worship of trees practiced here?" People looked at me in shock and then began telling me of the common practice of worshipping and even sacrificing to the *Mkuyu* (Sycamore Fig) tree and to the Baobab tree.[91] The day before, during a Bible study on Abraham's call in Genesis 12, we had talked about how leaving Haran, the place where Abraham's father Terah was buried, was a taboo in the ancient Near East. God's call took precedence over allegiance to tombs. Two individuals subsequently testified that they'd had dreams two years before where white men had come to tell them to stop worshipping graves and trees.

At other times, when we suddenly remember something that Jesus said or did, that's another sign that God, or more specifically the Holy Spirit, may be speaking. Jesus tells his disciples that a thought is divine communication when he says: "But the Helper, the Holy Spirit, whom the Father will send in my name, he will teach you all things, and *bring to your remembrance* all that I said to you" (Jn 14:15–16, emphasis mine).

To practice having God bring something to our remembrance, we can ask the Holy Spirit to remind us of something about Jesus, or to recall a miracle story that we've already read or heard. Elsewhere in Scripture, we are told to remember God's past actions as a way of staying conscious.[92] When a scene from the Gospels springs to mind, take note, for the Spirit may be at work.

91. See A. Werner, "The Galla of the East Africa Protectorate, Part II," in *Journal of the African Society,* no. 51, vol. 13 (April 1914): 286.

92. Dt 5:15; 7:8; 8:2; 15:15; 16:3; 24:18; Jgs 8:34; 1 Chr 16:12; Ps 77:11; 105:5; Mt 16:9; 2 Tm 2:8

God also guides our thoughts through the Spirit. When I prepare or lead Bible studies, I deliberately invite the Spirit to be my guide. Jesus tells his disciples that all believers will receive future revelation after he is gone: "I have many more things to say to you, but you cannot bear them now. But when he, the Spirit of truth, comes, he will guide you into all the truth; for he will not speak on his own initiative, but whatever he hears, He will speak; and he will disclose to you what is to come" (Jn 16:12–13).[93]

How might we experience the Spirit of truth coming to guide us[94]? Philip embodies this when he opens his mouth and begins speaking about Jesus as the suffering servant whom the Ethiopian eunuch reads about in Isaiah (Acts 8:31). Jesus promises that the Spirit will speak to believers whatever he hears from the Father. We can pray for and expect this guidance.

The Greek word for "disclose" (*anaggellō*) means to announce, inform, tell, providing "information, with the possible implication of considerable detail."[95] The Samaritan woman uses this word to describe what the Messiah will do: "he will declare [disclose] all things to us" (Jn 4:25). Jesus reveals himself to her as Messiah and Lord after disclosing many things to her (Jn 4:26).

In John's Gospel, Jesus reveals to his disciples how he is continually open to revelation from his Father:

"Truly, truly, I say to you, the Son can do nothing of himself, unless it is something he *sees the Father doing;* for whatever the Father does, these things the Son also does in like manner. For the Father loves the Son, and shows him all things that he himself is doing; and greater works than these will he show him, that you may marvel" (Jn 5:19–20).

This Scripture invites us into intimate communion with the Father, who is preparing even "greater works" for us to engage. Jesus calls us to learn to see, hear, and respond as he did:

93. See also Jn 16:14–15: "He will glorify me, for me will take of mine and will disclose it to you. All things that the Father has are mine; therefore I said that He takes of mine and will disclose it to you"

94. The Greek term for "guide" (*hodēgeō*) means to show the way, guide, lead.

95. J.P. Louw and Eugene Nida, eds., "Anaggello," in *Greek-English Lexicon of the New Testament,* Accordance Bible Software, 33.197.

"I can do nothing on my own initiative. *As I hear, I judge;* and my judgment is just, because I do not seek my own will, but the will of him who sent me" (Jn 5:30).

As we commune with God, we listen attentively to God's stirring, and we experiment as we step out in faith through the direction of the Holy Spirit.

In chapter seven, we will explore the place of meditation, prayer, and study in preparing Guerrilla Bible studies so we can encourage others to pursue God's living Word.

CHAPTER SEVEN

PREPARING GUERRILLA GOSPEL ENCOUNTERS

Life-changing engagement with the Bible flows out of a lifestyle of continual watchfulness and attentiveness to Jesus, our teacher and *comandanté*. We can actively seek the precious treasures of the kingdom that will bless us as and that we can share with others. As Jesus explains to his disciples while interpreting the parables he has been teaching to crowds by the sea: "Therefore every scribe who has become a disciple of the kingdom of heaven is like a head of a household, who brings out of his treasure things new and old" (Mt 13:52). When we pay attention to our own questions, deliberately seeking answers through prayer, study, and conversations with others, we often make exciting discoveries that we want to share. Our excitement and curiosity about Scripture will connect with, inspire, and motivate others.

Locating the treasure

How do we find treasures from the Bible that will inspire us and bless others? How do we know which particular biblical text to study in preparation for a Bible study, teaching, or sermon? Knowledge of the Bible combined with awareness of your personal journey, familiarity with the people you will be leading, and the social, economic, and political issues affecting them, along with sensitivity to the Spirit are all important parts of the discernment process.

I recommend daily personal reading of the Bible, ideally including the Psalms, another Old Testament reading, readings from the Gospels, and the epistles. The use of a daily lectionary or reading schedule that takes you through the entire Bible in one[96] or two years will expose you to a breadth of stories and biblical perspectives, giving you a wide pool of texts from which to draw.

I usually review and often use the readings from a lectionary such as the Revised Common Lectionary or the Catholic Mass Lectionary, which provides Sunday text selections that are aligned with the Christian liturgical calendar along with readings in three-year cycles of Year A, B, and C. Reading Psalms, Old Testament, Gospel, and epistle selections traditionally associated with Advent, Epiphany, Lent, Ascension, and Pentecost will keep you and your reading community remembering Jesus' life, death, resurrection, ascension, and the coming of the Spirit together with believers from Roman Catholic and many different mainline Protestant denominations around the world.

In your daily Bible reading, take note of verses that get your attention in particular ways. Note any questions that arise along with convictions, challenges, inspirations, and actions you feel led to take. Write down your thoughts and impressions. Let your personal reading guide your deeper pursuit of truth as you reflect on how you are being called to change in response to God's Word to you.

It takes a deliberate effort to read the Bible to illuminate your personal life and the larger world. "Your word is a lamp to my feet and a light to my path," writes the psalmist (Ps 119:105). Carlos Mesters comments that the light must not be stared at directly, but is meant to be aimed at reality like a flashlight on a path so as to illuminate our movement and action in the world. Swiss theologian Karl Barth reputedly advised young theologians "to take your Bible and take your newspaper, and read both. But interpret newspapers from your Bible."

The more you know your reading community and the individuals in your group, the more in tune you'll be with how to communicate a helpful message. Careful listening, knowledge of people's culture, social context, and particular challenges will help you choose relevant biblical texts to teach or discuss. If reading with active churchgoers, it is helpful to know what people have already and most recently been exposed to and

96. *One Year Bible: The Entire English Standard Version in 365 Daily Readings* (Wheaton: Tyndale, 1991).

something about their particular current challenges. If you are leading Bible studies in a homeless shelter or jail, you will likely have people who will be completely uninitiated to Christian faith.

The Apostle Paul models careful and contemplative reading of Scripture that is in tune with the needs of the individuals and faith communities that he is addressing and the pressing issues of his day. His letters draw from the Old Testament, his knowledge of Jesus, active relationship with the Holy Spirit, and his deep relationships with dispersed churches. May his words to his young disciple Timothy encourage and challenge you as you prepare to build people up in their faith: "Be diligent to present yourself approved to God as a workman who does not need to be ashamed, accurately handling the word of truth" (2 Tm 2:15).

INWARD PREPARATION AND SENSITIVITY TO THE SPIRIT

The first Psalm calls "blessed" the person who does not walk according to normal human counsel, but whose "delight is in the law [*Torah*][97] of the Lord and in his law he meditates day and night" (v. 2). Delight in God's word can be pursued through prayer, study, contemplative reading, and worship. Once we have tasted this delight, we will desire more, which can lead us into a continual, day and night contemplative pursuit of divine counsel. This pursuit will lead us to a blessed life. Psalm 1 goes on to say that the one who meditates on Scripture day and night will be "like a tree, planted by the streams of water, which yields its fruit in its season. And its leaf does not wither. And in whatever that one does they prosper" (v. 3). So how do we live more deeply into this lifestyle of watchful preparation?

Meditating on the word day and night (Ps 1) involves reflecting continuously on the rich treasures of spiritual truth revealed in Scripture and what they reveal about God. When we pray and worship, we address God directly in the second person (referring to God as "you"). Addressing God puts us in the presence of the One who reveals truth. We live as a

97. The Hebrew term *Torah*, which signifies the first five books of the OT, can also be translated as "teaching." The term *Torah* also refers to Israel's most sacred Scripture and could also mean Scripture or divine revelation.

disciple of the living Jesus when we speak directly to him, ask him questions, receive insights, and express gratitude. We can do this anytime.

But speaking directly to God—as Father, Son, and Holy Spirit—requires faith, and our faith will grow only as we exercise it. In fact, the Apostle Paul calls followers of Christ to pray without ceasing: "With all prayer and petition pray at all times in the Spirit" (Eph 6:18). Speaking to God and making specific requests (prayer and petition) will radically deepen our faith and our study of the Bible. Our meditation and prayer can become continual as we seek to nourish our spiritual hunger by following our curiosity and seeking answers to our questions.

For years I wondered how I could both mediate on Scripture day and night and also pray without ceasing. Then I realized that when I meditate on the Word, I often have insights that inspire me to commune with God through worship, lament, intercession, and other kinds of prayer. Those times of prayer lead me to reflect on God. Held together in this way, continual meditation and ceaseless prayer seem more possible.[98]

Ceaseless Meditation and Prayer

The word for meditate in Hebrew is *haga,* meaning moan, groan, murmur, utter, speak, or muse. *Haga* suggests deep engagement. Meditating is not so much an intellectual activity, but rather a deep ruminating, including a vocal or silent moaning or murmuring over the word.[99] When the Apostle Paul instructs us to "pray *in the Spirit* at all times" (Eph 6:18, emphasis mine), what exactly does this mean? In his epistle to the Romans, Paul connects this kind of prayer to Psalm 1. He says that "having the first fruits of the Spirit, even we ourselves groan within ourselves, waiting eagerly for our adoption as sons [and daughters]" (Rom 8:23). The term "groan" (*stenazo* in Greek) means "to sigh, murmur, pray inaudibly: — with grief, groan, grudge, sigh," which is quite similar to the Hebrew verb *haga.*[100]

98. See Daniel Bourguet, *Méditation de la Bible* (Lyon: Olivetan, 2000), 17

99. The Hebrew verb *haga.*

100. In the Septuagint of Ps 1, the Hebrew verb *haga* is matched with the Greek verb *meletaō*, which means "revolve in the mind: — imagine, (pre-) meditate" (Key Dictionary of Greek New Testament, Accordance Software) or "to care for, attend to carefully, practice" (Thayer, Accordance Software). See 1 Tm 4:15. (see Jos 1:8; Job 27:4; Ps 1:2; 2:1; 35:28; 37:30; 38:12; 63:6, and many more).

In verses 26–27, Paul makes this connection even more explicit: "In the same way the Spirit also helps our weakness; for we do not know how to pray as we should, but the Spirit himself intercedes for us with groanings (*stenagmos*) too deep for words."

Thus ceaseless praying in the Spirit is a kind of internal groaning that overlaps with meditation. We can engage in this ceaseless prayer and meditation "in the Spirit" when we are sleeping and also while we are working.[101] Continual meditation and ceaseless prayer in the spirit prepares us to receive prophetic revelation, which we will explore in the next section.

Prophetic Revelation

In Romans, Paul writes that when we are praying in the Spirit, and the Spirit intercedes for us with groanings too deep for words, we are brought into alignment with the Spirit's intercession for others: "He who searches the hearts knows what the mind of the Spirit is, because he intercedes for the saints according to the will of God" (Rom 8:27). In alignment with this, Paul follows his exhortation to pray in the spirit without ceasing with another imperative: "be on the alert with all perseverance and petition for all the saints" (Eph 6:18)—which includes the dimension of physical seeing, with an attitude of vigilance.[102] Praying in the spirit puts us into direct connection with God, who can and will inform us of the needs of individuals, the community, and world. Yet Paul also urges deliberate and persevering alertness regarding our intercession for others (petitions for all the saints). Intercession comes out of ceaseless prayer and attentiveness—foundational postures for sharing our faith through Bible study and proclamation.

As we prepare to proclaim God's word and salvation to others, Paul also urges us to pray for the gift of words spoken boldly in the face of persecution: "Pray on my behalf, that utterance may be given to me in

101. The Eastern Church fathers have written extensively on the possibility of ceaseless prayer, which they call the "prayer of the heart" or "the Jesus prayer."

102. *Agrupneō* means "To make an effort to learn of what might be a potential future threat — 'to be alert, to be on the lookout for, to be vigilant.'" J.P. Louw and Eugene Nida, eds., *Greek English Lexicon of the New Testament.* This term is often used to describe physical watching as with a sentry (LXX Ps 101:7; 126:1, and Prov 8:34).

the opening of my mouth, to make known with boldness the mystery of the gospel, for which I am an ambassador in chains; that in proclaiming it I may speak boldly, as I ought to speak" (Eph 6:19–20). Writing from prison as a guerrilla pastor par excellence, Paul reveals his dependency on God for prophetic revelation. He asks the community to whom he writes to pray that God will give him "utterance," using the term *logos* together with "in the opening of my mouth," which suggests speaking prophetically (Eph 6:19).[103] The persecuted Apostle knows he needs God to give him the capacity to make known the mystery of the gospel and to "speak boldly, as I ought to speak" (v. 19). Paul here points the way toward ceaseless meditation, prayer, and intercession that puts us in tune with the needs of individuals and communities, leading to contextually sensitive prophetic revelation. So how do we nurture this ceaseless communication?

Praying in the Spirit

Praying in the Spirit is synonymous with praying in tongues, which can be done both out loud and silently.[104] Speaking in tongues can also be practiced publicly for the benefit of listeners with interpretation. Praying in tongues or in the Spirit is direct communication with God. Tongues, or *glossolalia,* is directly associated with the baptism of the Spirit.

At the Feast of Pentecost, the Spirit comes upon the gathered believers, and a tongue alights on each one. This enables them to speak in other languages, which are recognizable to people gathered in Jerusalem from many nations. Whereas the gathered believers are speaking in tongues, bystanders hear them "speaking of the mighty deeds of God." (Acts 2:11). This does not necessarily mean that these uneducated disciples (who are referred to negatively as Galileans) are actually speaking foreign languages. According to the account, the people from different language groups "each hear them" in their own language, which suggests the possibility that the spiritual tongues may somehow include a translation to the

103. The "opening of the mouth" is an expression referring directly to human action in making ourselves available to receive and transmit a word from God (see Ez 3:2; 33:22; Ps 78:2; Acts 8:35; Mt 5:2; 13:35.

104. The only mention of praying in tongues is in 1 Cor 14:14, which states: "For if I pray in a tongue, my spirit prays, but my mind is unfruitful." Praying in the Spirit assumes a tripartite understanding of the human person, understood as having a body, soul, and spirit.

listeners (Acts 2:8). In public settings, Paul insists that for communication in tongues to benefit the community, there must be interpretation so that everyone can understand what is being said (1 Cor 14:27–28).

Speaking in tongues is also associated with the Spirit falling on Gentile listeners during Peter's preaching (Acts 10:45–47), which he later calls the "baptism with the Holy Spirit" (Acts 11:16). Speaking in tongues occurs again when the Holy Spirit comes on people after the Apostle Paul lays hands on them (Acts 19:6). Yet in these later cases, there is no mention of anyone understanding the tongues. The gift of tongues is a spiritual gift that enhances our personal communion with God: "For one who speaks in a tongue does not speak to people but to God; for no one understands, but in his spirit he speaks mysteries" (1 Cor 14:2). Paul goes on to say that "the one who speaks in a tongue edifies himself," depicting tongues as a personal prayer language that involves our spirit praying in a way distinct from our mind (v. 4). "For if I pray in a tongue, my spirit prays, but my mind is unfruitful" (v. 14).

Praying with our spirits does not replace the use of our minds and human language. This is not an either-or approach to meditation and prayer, but rather a both-and approach. As Paul himself continues: "What is the outcome then? I will pray with the spirit and I will pray with the mind also; I will sing with the spirit and I will sing with the mind also" (1 Cor 14:15). In the same way, we can meditate on Scripture with our spirits and our minds. As we pray in the Spirit, we can also pay attention to the people we are pastoring, the biblical text we are discussing and social problems and justice issues that need addressing.

A man recently shared with me how he grew up in a home where his mother took him and his siblings to church. His father grew up in a Catholic family, but he rejected the faith and had no interest in church. Over the years, this man pursued his father, seeking to talk with him about Jesus. His father resisted, even threatening to hang up when he talked about questions of faith. Finally, this man came to an impasse, not knowing how to engage his father. "I began to pray in tongues about my father, deliberately seeking to engage my mind, as Paul mentions in 1 Corinthians 14:14." Then he began to notice thoughts and pictures coming into his mind, which turned out to be prophetic revelations about his father's experiences in World War II and other life events. This man began to draw from these revelations in conversations with his father:

> I would be praying for him, speaking in tongues, and at the same time trying to engage my mind but in a way that was 'following' or 'tracking' with the Spirit. When I would finish praying I would be left with some 'impression', such as the nature of my Dad's relationship with his own father and with that came specific questions I felt I needed to ask him next time I called. As I try to explain this it sounds so very subjective but the kinds of impressions and questions that would come to me are not ones that I would have come up with on my own. I really believe they were from the Spirit. And when I would ask these particular questions they would have a remarkable effect on my Dad, softening him and making him more open to deeper conversations. They also led to a stronger bond between the two of us. Since this happened after decades of me not having any success in talking with my father about faith issues, I believe that this change, in the manner in which I prayed for him made all the difference.

Through prayer and conversation informed by the Holy Spirit, this man's father came to faith at the end of his life, much like the Samaritan woman who comes to believe after Jesus reveals that the man she is living with is not her husband and that she's had five husbands.

When we pray in the Spirit, we come to receive "things which eye has not seen and ear has not heard, and which have not entered the heart of people, all that God has prepared for those who love him" (1 Cor 2:9). In other words, revelation that is inaccessible through normal human seeing and hearing are available to us from God through the Holy Spirit. In the same way that the Spirit searches people's hearts, the Spirit of God knows God's mind and will reveal God's thoughts to those who love him (Rom 8:27). As Paul writes in his first epistle to the Corinthians: "For to us God revealed them through the Spirit; for the Spirit searches all things, even the depths of God… Even so the thoughts of God no one knows except the Spirit of God" (2:10–11).

Once, as I prepared to minister to imprisoned gang members in Guatemala, I was warned that there was tremendous resistance and even antagonism towards Christians who insisted that gang members had to leave their gang to follow Jesus. Gang members who leave their gangs after becoming Christians were being killed, because churches are viewed as rival gangs. As I was being transported from Guatemala City to lead Bible studies with MS-13 gang members[105] in a maximum security prison, I prayed in silently in tongues, asking for wisdom about how to talk about Jesus' call of the tax-collector, Matthew, who left his tax booth to follow Jesus. As I prayed, the following question came to mind: "Who followed whom after Jesus called Matthew?" I looked at the passage in Mark 2:14–15 and saw that after Matthew got up and followed Jesus, they went to Matthew's house, where they dined with many tax collectors and sinners.

While leading the Bible study on Mark 2:14–17 inside the prison, I asked the gang members whether Matthew had to leave his gang when Jesus called him. The men all looked at me in silence, expecting to hear the bad news that they, like Matthew, would have to leave their gang if they followed Jesus. I then invited someone to read Mark 2:15, asking people to pay attention to where Jesus and Matthew went after Matthew decided to follow Jesus: "And it happened that he was reclining at the table in his house, and many tax collectors and sinners were dining with Jesus and his disciples; for there were many of them, and they were following him." When the men saw that Jesus had followed Matthew to his house, they were astounded. I turned to the leader of the gang and asked him if he could see himself welcoming Jesus in his barrio, into his gang? This insight into the text was a gift from the Holy Spirit that led to a spiritual breakthrough.

As we prepare to preach, lead Bible studies, and teach, we need to remember that revelation is a gift of God through the Spirit that is available to all. As Paul exhorts the church at Corinth: "Now we have received, not the spirit of the world, but the Spirit who is from God, so that we may know the things freely given to us by God" (1 Cor 2:12). Preparing and facilitating guerrilla Bible studies involves communion with Jesus,

105. The MS-13 gang, otherwise known as Mara Salvatrucha or simple MS, is an international criminal gang that originated in Los Angeles, California in the 1980s. The gang later spread to many parts of the continental United States, Canada, Mexico, and Central America, and is active in urban and suburban areas. Most members are ethnically of Central American origin (principally El Salvador).

our rabbi, commander, and primary source. As we live in the power of the Spirit of Christ, we "speak, not in words taught by human wisdom, but those taught by the Spirit, combining spiritual thoughts and spiritual words" (1 Cor 2:13).

Jesus promises that he will send those who follow him the Holy Spirit, who he calls the Advocate, to help us in our pursuit of divine revelation: "He will teach you all things, and bring to your remembrance all that I said to you" (Jn 14:26). Jesus calls the Holy Spirit "the Spirit of truth" and says that the Spirit comes from the Father to "testify about me" (Jn 15:26). He also says that the Holy Spirit "will lead you into all truth" (Jn 16:13). When we invite the Holy Spirit to guide us as we read and study the Bible, the epistle ascribed to the Apostle James promises us that we can expect revelation: "But if any of you lacks wisdom, let him ask of God, who gives to all generously and without reproach, and it will be given to him" (Jas 1:5). The writer of this epistle adds: "But he must ask in faith without any doubting," urging believers to resist skepticism and expect answers (Jas 1:6).

One way to enter God's presence before studying Scripture is to give thanks. I often ask the Holy Spirit to remind me of answers to prayer or recent unsolicited blessings. Then I write down a list of thanksgivings in my journal, alongside petitions that are on my heart, as well as a to-do list. Then I deliberately give thanks to God for everything on the list along with other gratitudes that come to mind. In this way, worship comes naturally, as the psalmist writes: "Enter his presence with thanksgiving and his courts with praise" (Ps 100:4). Then I pray through each of my petitions.

When preparing to lead a Bible study, I ask the Holy Spirit to illuminate my reading of a particular passage and give me understanding. I dialogue with God in response to challenges that arise from the text. Then I give thanks for any insights that emerge. Right before I go to sleep at night, I re-read the passage and ask the Spirit to give me revelation in the night. I keep a journal beside my bed to write down whatever comes. Following are other meditational practices that I find helpful in preparing to lead Bible studies.

Praying the Word: Lectio Divina

Lectio Divina is an ancient Christian practice of praying the Word of God. There are many ways to pray Scripture. One way is to read the entire passage over prayerfully, expecting revelation. As you read, take note of what jumps out at you and use this to launch into prayer. Then re-read each verse with thanksgiving, interceding for people or asking for understanding.

For example, after reading John 4:6, where "Jesus, being wearied from His journey, was sitting thus by the well. . . about the sixth hour," I felt inspired and prayed, "Jesus, thank you for letting us see that you too became weary as you traveled and had to rest. Thank you also for showing us that you, being God, showed up ahead of the Samaritan woman. You were already there at the hour when she arrived to draw water. You were there in weakness as a tired Jewish man in a foreign place. Help me to identify you in the ordinary places, in your weakness and vulnerability."

GUIDE TO INTERPRETING BIBLICAL TEXTS

There are many helpful step-by-step guides to assist you in studying Scripture and preparing to lead Bible studies.[106] Gerald West offers a useful distinction between three modes of reading the Bible, which he calls "[the world] behind the text," "in front of the text," and "the text itself."[107] Following are brief descriptions of each of these modes.

Behind the Text Mode

The "world behind the text" mode emphasizes reconstructing the original historical and sociological context in order to determine what the original author was trying to communicate to their audience.[108] Historical background information that is not present in the Bible can be very important for interpreting biblical texts that address problems

106. Gordon D. Fee, Douglas Stewart, *How to Read the Bible for All Its Worth* (Grand Rapids: Zondervan, 1981).

107. Gerald West, *Contextual Bible Study* (Pietermaritzburg: Cluster, 1993), 28

108. Source criticism, form criticism, redaction criticism, and socio-historical interpretation are included in this category of 'behind the text.'

known to the original addressees but not to our culture and context. Research into the historical background underlying many of Paul's comments about women,[109] slavery, homosexuality,[110] submission to governing authorities, and other topics clarifies biblical texts that have been used to suppress people.

In Front of the Text Mode

The "in front of the text" mode is "reader-centered" rather than focusing on the author's original intent or analyzing the text itself. The reader comes to Scripture with a particular question or concern, such as "advocacy for the poor," "hearing God's voice," or "healing in the Bible." This topic or question of interest is placed "in front of the text" as an interpretive key. Then a book or section of Scripture is studied in pursuit of relevant perspectives.[111] West describes the value of this kind of reading:

> So readers merge or fuse their world with the world of the text through a process of dialogue with the text. In this process of dialogue between the questions, needs, and interests of the readers and the themes, metaphors, and symbols of the text both the reader and the text are transformed. When readers enter the world of the text it transforms them by providing a new way of seeing and being; it offers them new possibilities. When the world of the reader is brought to the text it transforms the text by allowing a plurality of possible readings not perceived in the past to be appropriated in the present by the reader; it offers the text a new way of speaking.[112]

One disadvantage of an "in front of the text" approach includes the difficulties that untrained readers might encounter in identifying key texts on a given topic. Another disadvantage arises when we limit our

109. See John T. Bristow, *What Paul Really Said About Women: The Apostle's Liberating Views on Equality in Marriage, Leadership and Love* (New York: HarperCollins, 1988), Lucy Peppiatt, *Women and Worship at Corinth: Paul's Rhetorical Arguments in 1 Corinthians* (Eugene: Cascade Books, 2015).

110. William J. Webb, *Slaves, Women and Homosexuals: Exploring the Hermeneutics of Cultural Analysis* (Downers Grove: IVP Academic, 2001).

111. See West, *Contextual Bible Study*, 41–47.

112. Ibid., 44.

Bible reading to verses that address particular themes in a pre-critical way rather than reflecting on the breadth of the biblical narrative.[113]

Text-based Mode

A text-based mode concentrates on reading the final version of the biblical text carefully in its literary context, paying attention to characters, language, and how the text is structured. Careful reading of the text requires continuous practice and training. However, text-based reading is possible as long as people have access to Bibles and are willing to learn careful reading practices. In the following guide to biblical interpretation, I focus on reading the final version of the biblical text. I will also use an "in front of the text" mode of reading, which is more accessible than a "behind the text" approach.

Determine where your text begins and ends

Once you decide the biblical text you want to study, the next step is to look more closely at the final version of the text. First determine more precisely where your selection of Scripture begins and ends. Unlike our versions of the Bible today, Scripture was originally written without punctuation. In the original Hebrew, Aramaic, and Greek biblical manuscripts, there were no chapter or verse divisions. These were added much later so that people could find their way around the books of the Bible.[114] While current chapters and verses often accurately reflect natural starting and stopping places, it's best to get in the habit of determining the beginning and ending places yourself.

Even when you find a natural beginning place, it is important to keep in mind that stories or topical teachings in the Bible are connected chronologically or thematically to what comes before and after. They are part of a larger story or, in the case of an epistle, they are inside the body of a letter to a particular community. Ideally try to read the chapters surrounding your chosen text. You will learn to identify digestible sections to preach, teach, or lead people through dialogically. Be sure to

113. Ibid., 46–47 for a fuller discussion of advantages and disadvantages.

114. The English Cardinal of the Roman Catholic Church and the Archbishop of Canterbury is credited with organizing Scripture into the current arrangement of chapters between 1207 and 1228.

take notes about anything that seems to clarify the meaning of your text as you're reading.

As you read, try to identify a section of Scripture that is the right length for your audience based on their educational background, age, attention span, prior knowledge of the Bible, exposure to Christianity, as well as the amount of time you have. If you are doing a bilingual Bible study, plan for twice as much time since the text must be read and discussed in two languages. Reading a couple of verses closely is better than being overambitious and biting off more than time allows. In our weekly jail Bible studies, we are limited to thirty-minute gatherings, which includes greetings, introductions, music, prayer, and ministry time. This limits our studies to between five and eight verses, though sometimes I may focus on only one or two verses.

When focusing on a limited number of verses, it is important to determine natural starting and ending points for different sections of a story or biblical teaching. Following is a helpful guide to assist you in dividing biblical narratives into natural and workable sections.

First, read through the section of Scripture, trying to determine natural starting and ending points based on details in the text. Notice the characters, their location, actions, and words. As an example, we can look again at the story of Jesus' encounter with the Samaritan woman in John 4. The story naturally begins with Jesus' departure from Judea that brings him into Samaria (vv. 3–4) and ends when Jesus leaves Samaria for Cana in Galilee (v. 43–45).

Second, read through the verses in your selected text, breaking it down into smaller sections. Jesus' encounter with the Samaritan woman is far too long for a thirty- to forty-five-minute Bible study. But this larger narrative can be broken down into several scenes, as described in the following. Verses 1–6 set the scene. Verses 7–15 describe Jesus' first conversation with the Samaritan woman, and she asks for living water. In verses 16–26, Jesus reveals the woman's marital status and personal history; the woman identifies Jesus as a prophet, questions him about the "right" place of worship, and then Jesus' reveals himself as Messiah. In verse 27, the disciples return to Jesus. In verses 28–30, the woman leaves her pot at the well, returns to Sychar to share about her experience with Jesus, and then the people of the village come to him at the well. In verses 31–38, Jesus speaks with his disciples about food, God's will, and the harvest. In verses 39–42, the people of the city of Sychar believe in Jesus, he stays for two days among them, and many believe.

Third, once you have decided natural starting and ending points for a particular passage, read the sections of Scripture before and after your chosen text in order to understand the narrative in light of the immediate literary context. For example, prior to the Samaritan narrative, a Pharisee leader named Nicodemus comes to Jesus by night, and they talk about new birth (John 3:1–21). This dialogue is followed by descriptions of Jesus' baptizing activity (vv. 22–24), discussions between John's disciples and a Jew about purification (v. 25), and by John the Baptist's final testimony about Jesus' superiority (vv. 26–36). After Jesus' encounter with the Samaritan woman in John 4:7–45, a royal official from Capernaum comes to Jesus in Cana, asking him to heal his son, and Jesus heals the boy from a distance (John 4:46–54).

Fourth, try to read the bigger story in the chapters surrounding the selected passage of Scripture, asking how your text fits within the larger story of that book of the Bible. If you have time, it might be helpful to read that whole book, outlining the major sections and topics, so that you understand how the text relates to the larger narrative, which is called the "broad literary context."

For example, Jesus' encounter with the Samaritan woman in John 4 is located in the midst of a long narrative section presenting Jesus' ministry and teaching in Judea and Galilee (Jn 1:19-12:50), which includes his performing of seven miraculous signs ending with his raising of Lazarus from the dead (Jn 11:1-45). This leads Jewish religious authorities to plot to kill him, transitioning to a long narrative section on Jesus' final days into Jerusalem. In Jerusalem he celebrates the Last Supper with his disciples, and then he is arrested, crucified and raised from the dead (John 13:1-20:31). John's Gospel ends with descriptions of his appearances and final words to his disciples after his resurrection and his ascension (21:1-25).

Fifth, consider where your text is located within the whole Bible. Locating your text in the "canonical context" helps you understand how it relates to the larger story of God moving throughout the biblical narrative.

Jesus' encounter with the Samaritan woman in John 4 is located in the fourth and final gospel account of the life, death, resurrection and ascension of Jesus. John's Gospel is preceded by the synoptic gospel accounts of Matthew, Mark and Luke, which launch the New Testament Scriptures. John's Gospel is followed by Acts of the Apostles, which recount the launching of the Jesus movement beginning at Pentecost and continuing to Samaria and the ends of the earth through Paul's Gentile mission. Paul's Epistles, the pastoral epistles and the book of Revelation make up the rest of the New Testament. The New Testament presents Jesus as God's Son, Israel's Messiah and the world's Savior—who fulfills the Old Testament Scriptures.

The Old Testament begins with the Torah (Genesis-Deuteronomy), which recounts the origins of God's liberation movement, beginning with the creation of the world, and human beings as God's image bearers (Gen 1), the call of Israel's founding couple Abram and Sarai, the establishment of the twelve tribes of Israel, liberation of God's people from slavery in Egypt, and the giving of the Law. The Prophets include the conquest of Canaan, the establishment of Israel as a nation, the construction of the Temple in Jerusalem, the exile of God's people by the Assyrians and Babylonians, and their return to the land and rebuilding of the temple. In the Prophets and Writings Israel is repeatedly called to be God's missionary people and promised a Messiah-Savior-King who would establish an eternal Kingdom. John presents Jesus as God's Word made flesh who reveals the Father, the Messiah and perfect embodiment of Israel's vocation to announce and accomplish salvation to the world.

Sixth, with all the information you've gathered, discern which verses to concentrate on and the most relevant sections of the narrative that precede and follow that passage. At this point in the interpretative process it is helpful to print out a hard copy of the text to highlight and take notes on, which you can refer to as you continue to meditate on the Scripture and prepare to lead a Bible study.

Once you have decided to study a particular text, find a place where you won't be distracted and re-read each verse several times, asking the Spirit for wisdom, inspiration, and revelation. Though it can be challenging and intimidating to discern the meaning of a text that was written thousands of years ago to ancient people who spoke foreign languages and were culturally different, relax, pray, and anticipate God speaking to you as you read. Recall the steps to hearing God's voice discussed in chapter five: quiet yourself down; look for vision; tune into spontaneity; write it down. As you read, pay attention to the following questions: *What seems clear to you in the text? What is most relevant to your life? to your reading community? to the world? What surprises you or delights you? What questions do you need answered in order to better understand this passage?*

Compare Different Translations

Since the original languages of the Old Testament are Hebrew and Aramaic, and the New Testament was written in Greek, you will most likely be working from a translation into your own language. For your study, I suggest choosing a translation that is as literal as possible to the underlying Hebrew or Greek original, but still uses familiar English or the language in which you are working. It is best to avoid versions that paraphrase. Choose at least two good translations for comparison, including versions that are available to the people with whom you read.[115]

As you read your text in two (or more) translations, take note of any significant differences, which can alert you to translation difficulties that can be pursued later through commentaries or online resources.

The following story gives an example about the importance of referring to more than one translation. For years, I was troubled by Jesus' teaching in Matthew 10:29, which in the Revised Standard Version reads: "Are not two sparrows sold for a penny? And not one of them will fall to the ground *without your Father's will.*" This verse appears to support the theology that death is God's sovereign will rather than the last enemy to be destroyed (see 1 Cor 15:26). However, in comparing this translation to the New American Standard Version, I noticed a significant difference: "And *yet* not one of them will fall to the ground apart from your Father." This led me to search the underlying Greek word, and I learned that there

115. I recommend English translations such as the NASB, ESV, RSV, NRSV, NIV, NKJV, NJB.

is no underlying Greek equivalent to "will of"—and so this translation reflects the theology of the RSV translator.

Consider Literary Details

After comparing two or more translations, read through the text slowly and carefully, paying attention to the following literary considerations. What is the literary style of the Biblical text you are reading? If you are reading poetry, which makes up thirty-three percent of the Bible and is found in the Psalms, wisdom literature and in the resistance oracles in the prophets, it is especially important to pay close attention to who is speaking to or about whom, and many other details. Prose discourse makes up around twenty-four percent of the Bible, including speeches, essays and letters—like Paul's epistles and the pastoral epistles. Forty-three percent of Scripture consists of narrative.[116] Since these are real life stories they are usually for untrained readers to access.

First, identify the different characters in the text. What do we know about each character from the larger story surrounding the text? What does each character say or do? Who is speaking to or about whom? Does the speaker or audience change? Second, where is the story or text located geographically or spatially? Pay attention to the names of places. Does the location change from start to finish? If so, might this signify something noteworthy? Third, what happens in the text? What is the central action? Can you trace the plot? Pay particular attention to verbs and subjects of verbs. Finally, consider your own contemporary equivalents to these literary details. What might these people, this place, these buildings look like in your community or for those with whom you are reading?

Paying careful attention to these literary details will help you slow down and focus on what is actually taking place in the text. It is important to slow down, reflect, and take stock of who the characters are, what they represent, and what each one says and does. Try to identify personally with the characters, putting yourself in their places. Who do you most identify with in this story and why? Where can you identify similar characters in your own life and in the society around you?

116. See https://thebibleproject.com/explore/how-to-read-the-bible/

Locate the Story Center (Turning Point)

Biblical stories are often carefully organized around a center, which is often the turning point in a story, poem or prose discourse text. Read and re-read through the text, looking for key points where shifts take place. To locate the story center for a particular passage, consider the following questions: *What changes from beginning to end? What is the text organized to say? What is the main idea of the passage and where is it communicated within the text?*

In considering the story of Jesus' encounter with the Samaritan woman and the villagers of Sychar, we observe that the story is book-ended by the reasons for Jesus' departure from Judea to Sychar (Jn 4:1–4) and his movement from Sychar towards Galilee (v. 43). The story begins and ends with Jesus as he leaves both places. His lone encounter with a single Samaritan woman is highlighted at the center. In the opening scene, Jesus is outside the city at a well, asking the lone Samaritan woman for hospitality (a drink of water), which she refuses to give him (vv. 6–7). By the end of the account, Jesus is invited by inhabitants of the city to spend two days there, and many come to believe because of his word, stating their conviction that he is the Savior of the world (vv. 40–42).

Moving deeper into the story, when the woman asks Jesus how he, being a Jew, can ask her, a Samaritan woman, for a drink, Jesus offers her living water. At first she questions this offer, but eventually she asks Jesus to give her some of this water. He responds by asking her to bring her husband—and then reveals that the man she's living with is not her husband and that she's had five previous husbands. This revelation leads the woman to recognize Jesus as a prophet (vv. 9–19). Towards the end of the story, the narrator tells us that many Samaritans believed in Jesus because of the woman's testimony: "he told me all the things that I have done." This leads them to invite Jesus to stay with them (vv. 39–40).

Moving still deeper towards the center of the story, we see that the Samaritan woman tells Jesus that her people's fathers worshipped on "this mountain," whereas Jews worship in Jerusalem. Jesus tells her that the hour is coming, and now is, when true worshippers will worship the Father in spirit and truth. The woman states her expectation that Messiah is coming, who will tell her and her people all things (vv. 20–25). Towards the end of the story, we see Jesus refuse to eat the food his disciples have brought him from the city because he says he's already eaten, for his food is to do his Father's work. He speaks of fields already white for harvest and of the one who reaps already receiving wages and gathering fruit for eternal life (vv. 31–38).

At the center of the story, Jesus reveals to the woman that he is the Messiah (v. 26), simultaneously identifying himself as the Lord by using the same words, *ego eimi,* that God uses when he reveals his name to Moses in Exodus 3:14. Jesus' self-disclosure as God identifies him with the Father, suggesting that "the hour now is" when true worshipers will worship the Father in spirit and truth. Jesus' revelation coincides with the disciples' return from Sychar (v. 27). The woman leaves her water jar at the well and goes into the city, telling the inhabitants to come and see a man who has told her everything she's ever done and asking, "could this be the Messiah?" (vv. 28–29). The people come out to him at the well (v. 30). In this story, the people worship in spirit and in truth, and the one who sows and the one who reaps rejoice together. The disciples (and future readers) witness this revolutionary encounter.

Consider Word Meaning

As you study the biblical passage, pay careful attention to words you are drawn to because you are curious about their meanings. In order to properly study the meaning of words and their use in a particular book or in the Bible as a whole, you will need to know the underlying Hebrew or Greek word. This can be done through Hebrew or Greek-English interlinear Bibles, Bible software programs,[117] or online resources.[118]

Once you've identified the underlying Hebrew or Greek word, use Hebrew and Greek-English lexicons and concordances (or Bible app,[119]

117. Accordance Bible Software, Version 11.0.3, OakTree Software Inc, November 2014, Logos Bible Software.

118. A helpful online resource for word searches and study notes is Blue Letter Bible (www.blueletterbible.org). For video overviews of the entire Bible, see www.thebibleproject.com. For a good Hebrew-English online interlinear translation, see http://www.scripture4all.org/OnlineInterlinear/Hebrew_Index.htm. For a Greek-English New Testament online interlinear translation, see http://www.scripture4all.org/OnlineInterlinear/Greek_Index.htm.

119. Olive Tree Bible Software or Glo Bible provide helpful apps.

Bible software programs, or online resources) to look for word meanings and other occurrences of the word in the book and elsewhere in Scripture. The goal here is to determine how key words and images are used in your text.

Meanings of words are best determined by first considering the range of dictionary meanings, looking at how the word is used in the immediate context of the verses and also in the larger book (and the Bible as a whole). Comparing translations can also help you see how other translators have translated certain words.

Intertextual Interpretation

The most common form of biblical interpretation used in ancient times is often called intertextual exegesis. Biblical authors used words that deliberately linked their text to the same word in another part of Scripture. When we study New Testament texts, we must remember that the Old Testament used and cited by Greek-writing New Testament authors was usually the Septuagint, the ancient Greek translation of the Old Testament. In order to identify deliberate links between New Testament and Old Testament stories, you must search for the usages of the New Testament Greek word in the Septuagint. You can learn how to do word searches in the Septuagint through concordances and the Bible software programs mentioned above. Online resources are also available for searching the Septuagint, and a good English translation of the Septuagint is readily available.[120]

For example, in studying Jesus' encounter with the Samaritan woman at the well in John 4, the passage uses two words for "well". The first term, *pege* (spring), occurs when Jesus sits beside the spring when he first meets the woman in verse 6 and again in verse 11, when the woman tells Jesus that the well is deep and he has nothing to draw the water. The second term, *phrear* (cistern), is used in verse 12 when the woman refers to her ancestor Jacob's well.[121] Through a word search in the Septuagint, I found a link between the spring, *pege*, in John 4:6 and 4:11, the *pege* where the

120. Lancelot C. Brenton, *The Septuagint with Apocrypha: Greek and English* (Grand Rapids: Zondervan, 1973).

121. *Phrear* is used in Jn 4:11, 12, and elsewhere in the NT in Lk 14:5; Rev 9:1–2.

angel of the Lord finds Hagar in Genesis 16:7, and the *pege* where Abraham's servant finds a wife for Isaac (Rebekkah, Jacob's mother) in Genesis 24:13ff. This intertextual link directly associates Jesus with the angel of the Lord and also with Abraham's servant. When Jesus offers to give the Samaritan woman a "spring of water leaping up to eternal life" (Jn 4:14), she—and we, as readers—are invited to remember these divinely orchestrated encounters at wells.

Consider Historical Background

Studying the historical background of your biblical text can also provide helpful insights. Knowing something about the author, addressees, and the socio-historical realities of the times can help you reconstruct the original context, imagining how people might have once interpreted the text. There are many scholarly commentaries and resources that discuss questions of authorship, date, and place. However, since we are thousands of years from the original settings, much historical-critical interpretation rests on hypothetical reconstructions of ancient history.

I place a lower priority on "behind the text" approaches since most readers of Scripture do not have access to libraries where they can find this kind of information. Drawing from this kind of background information can intimidate people who are not formally educated, disempowering untrained readers who already may feel unqualified to interpret Scripture.[122] There is so much insight to be gained through reading biblical texts carefully in their immediate literary context and in the larger context of Scripture that I prefer to see people put their energies there

122. Gerald West adds that "ordinary readers may feel there is a danger that the community might become dependent on or manipulated by outside 'expert' input. Even if training and resources were available and accessible, there is still a disadvantage in the approach because facilitators and their churches and communities would have no role in the production of this knowledge; in other words, were the knowledge available and accessible it would still be 'outside' knowledge, and not knowledge derived from their context and experience. Ordinary readers also feel that a behind the text mode of reading might sometimes create too much of a gap between the past of the text and the present of their context. In addition, because the historical and sociological background information provided by this mode of reading is often conflicting, this might result in confusion and inaction on the part of ordinary readers" (West, *Contextual Bible Study*, 34).

first. However, historical background information—when available—can be interesting.

Knowing about the background of the conflict between Jews and Samaritans helped me appreciate Jesus' rule breaking. Most of this information was available within Scripture itself, but scholarly commentaries also proved helpful. When studying about the exact location of Sychar, I learned that there's good scholarly evidence that Sychar was the same place as Shechem. This helped me see a link between Jesus and his twelve disciples and Jacob and his twelve sons, which ties John 4 directly to the story of the rape of Jacob's daughter, Dinah, in Genesis 34, as discussed in chapter four.

Consult Exegetical Commentaries

When possible, consult exegetical commentaries on the text you are studying. However, I encourage you to do this *after* you've done your own research so that you will not be deprived of the joy of making your own discoveries. Most scholarly commentators may overlook contextually sensitive insights that you will be able to make through the inspiration of the Spirit. At the same time, some of your insights may need to be corrected by more experienced and trained interpreters. When studying Old Testament texts, consider how Jewish,[123] New Testament authors, and early Christian interpreters understood your passage.

Summarize Findings

Once you have completed a close study of the biblical text, write a one-paragraph summary of the passage to clarify the Bible study for yourself and your audience. Then write up a verse-by-verse commentary to draw together what you've learned. This is a valuable process that often brings greater clarity and new insights. In order to write this commentary, you will need to make decisions about discoveries you have made based on translations, literary style, literary structure, historical context, and other considerations.

123. Included in ancient Jewish interpretation are the Septuagint, the Targums, Babylonian Talmud, Jerusalem Talmud, and Midrash.

Lead Guerrilla Bible Studies

The best way to deepen your understanding of a biblical passage is to lead a Bible study, teach, or preach from that text! As you share insights from your study, more insights will likely come. Other people's comments and questions will further enrich your understanding. In chapter eight, we will look at the dynamics of facilitating guerrilla Bible studies.

CHAPTER EIGHT

AGENTS OF LIBERATION: THE ART OF HOSTING GUERRILLA GOSPEL ENCOUNTERS

Facilitating transformational Bible studies can be a beautiful and complex process that is more of an art than a science, with nearly endless variations for reading, discussing, and responding to Scripture. Your approach in leading guerrilla gospel encounters will vary according to your personality, context, and each participant's background, immediate needs, level of education, and familiarity with the Bible, along with the relational dynamics you have developed as a group. The goal of the gospel encounter is for everyone to be drawn to God in and through Jesus, who wants to meet, love, free, transform, and recruit each of us to become agents of holistic liberation. You are a facilitator of this liberating process as you engage the biblical text along with the group, guided and empowered by the Holy Spirit.

In the Gospels we see how Jesus relates to individuals and groups in many different ways, often combining direct encounters and conversations around biblical texts and Jewish traditions with advocacy, healing, casting out evil spirits, and other prophetic actions. We can learn from Jesus and the Apostles' examples as we are humbly led by the Holy Spirit to express and demonstrate God's unconditional love.

Facilitating guerrilla gospel encounters or Bible studies is somewhat like hosting a banquet for people who aren't used to being invited to formal dinners. In Luke's account a man prepares a big dinner and invites many. After his first invitees offer excuses he tells his slave: "'Go out at once into the streets and lanes of the city and bring in here the poor and crippled and blind and lame.' And the slave said, 'Master, what you commanded has been done, and still there is room.' And the master said to the slave, 'Go out into the highways and along the hedges, and compel them to come in, so that my house may be filled'" (Lk 14:21–23). In Matthew's account, Jesus compares the Kingdom of God to a marriage feast, where invitees are not willing to attend, pay no attention to the king's slaves who invite them, and finally mistreat and kill the message bearers (Mt 22:6). This brutal action prompts the king to send out more slaves, saying: 'The wedding is ready, but those who were invited were not worthy. Go therefore to the main highways, and as many as you find there, invite to the wedding feast' (Mt 22:8).

In the same way, as facilitators, we invite and welcome people, and find that those we pursue are too busy, disinterested or even outright hostile. Forewarned by this parable, we persist in our inviting, focusing deliberately on those whom God chooses, paying close attention to the master's precise instructions about where to find the guests. The slaves (facilitators) are sent to pursue those who are normally excluded and bring them in to celebrate at the feast. Their inclusive invitations transgress normal societal and religious rules and oppose the dominant theology of the landowners (the ones who hold the power). The final section of this parable in Matthew's account describes an imposter inside the group, who is discovered and thrown out—an unpleasant intervention that some facilitators may have to enact in order to protect the "chosen" guests of the King (Mt 22:13).

Facilitators are also like the disciples in the miracle of the multiplication of the loaves and fish, available to help Jesus as he teaches. When Jesus has compassion for the crowds, they respond to his instructions by locating the existing resources within the crowd (five loaves and two fish) and bringing them to Jesus, who blesses them. Then they organize the people into groups, as Jesus indicates, and distribute the provisions until everyone has more than enough (Mk 6:33–44).

Facilitators can also be compared with the servants who do what Jesus commands in his first miracle at the wedding feast in Cana. When the wine runs out, Jesus orders the servants to fill up the water jugs with water and bring some to the headwaiter, which turns into the finest wine en route. This example suggests that following Jesus' instructions may not make rational sense but will require faith. Our primary role is to serve Jesus, the behind-the-scenes host, attending to his instructions in order to bless people with lavish provision.

Drawing on another metaphor, facilitating a Bible study can also be like midwifing a baby. The group is like a laboring mother, and the facilitator assists her in the most natural way possible. Effective facilitation involves spiritual midwifery—using your knowledge of the Bible, pastoral sensitivity, and interpersonal skills to accompany the group in bringing forth a timely word from God.

The facilitator sets up the birthing room, working in harmony with co-facilitators, to make sure the space is safe, secure, and comfortable and to prepare the expectant group. The facilitator models respectful and attentive listening, an encouraging and empowering presence, and sensitive coaching and guidance. The facilitator also assures that in an emergency situation, intervention will be swift and effective. Interventions might include keeping things moving by asking guiding questions, gently directing a conversation away from legalistic interpretations and conflicts, and offering clarity at critical moments. The facilitator humbly recognizes when he or she does not have answers, modeling an openness to seek expert advice when needed from those with more knowledge or experience.

After the birth, the facilitator cleans off the "newborn" word from God, ensures it has sufficient oxygen (clarification), and makes sure the "parents" know how to care for it in its vulnerable state. Finally, the facilitator provides regular checkups to ensure healthy growth, connecting the group to additional resources as needed.

BECOMING AN AGENT OF LIBERATION

Before you begin facilitating Bible studies, it's important for you to know your community by carefully listening and observing the people with whom you hope to minister. Further study may be necessary to help you understand the background and current situation of the people. Following are some general guidelines for becoming an effective guerrilla Bible study facilitator.

Embody God's Love

As facilitators, we are mediators who embody God's tender, unconditional love.[124] Our primary objective is to facilitate an encounter between Jesus and the individuals with whom we read. This encounter is mediated through the Bible and ourselves. Jesus says that when people receive us, they are receiving him, as well as the Father who sent him. Jesus never pressures or manipulates people to follow him, but loves people without strings. Some people may have encountered Christians who don't care about them as individuals, but only about their decisions for salvation. When we demonstrate care for people as individuals, asking them about their lives, responding to their concerns, offering to pray for them and their families, and following up with them when possible, our care builds trust and heals wounds that may have been inflicted by conditional acceptance experienced elsewhere.

Identify Barriers to Relationship

Our unique identities and backgrounds can create many obstacles, depending on the subculture(s) of our reading communities. Consider prejudices people might have about us—or ones they expect us to have about them—around factors such as race, gender, class, national identity, culture, political party, religion, and denomination, and how we may need to work to overcome some of these negative expectations.[125] We each need to regularly re-discover and re-affirm our baptismal identity, dying to distinctives of our flesh, so that our status as God's son or daughter will take precedence in all our engagements with people.[126] We can lower "us–them" barriers and seek to optimize trust and empowerment with our group by being authentic, humble, and interested in the people,

124. See Daniel Bouguet, *The Tenderness of God* (Eugene: Cascade Books, 2017).

125. See Bob Ekblad, "Reading Scripture for Good News Across Barriers of Race/Ethnicity, Class and Culture," *Multicultural Perspectives on Reading the Bible, Interpretation: A Journal of Bible and Theology* 65, no. 3 (July 2011): 229–248.

126. See Bob Ekblad, *A New Christian Manifesto*, 32-51.

carrying ourselves in ways that do not reinforce insecurities, especially assumptions about inferiority.

For example, in my work as a jail chaplain, I serve prisoners from a wide range of racial and class backgrounds, including low-income and working-class Caucasians, Mexicans, Chicanos, and Native Americans. Prisoners will usually assume that I consider myself superior to them, am in agreement with the State regarding their charges, imprisonment, and sentencing, and that I am a moralistic and judgmental Christian (which may be all they've ever experienced), and that I represent mainstream White American values. In my efforts to represent Jesus as an ambassador for the Kingdom of God, I often look for ways to differentiate myself naturally so as to challenge people's prejudices and insecurities.

Yet our motivation as facilitators should never be to prove that we are sensitive, politically correct, cross-cultural experts worthy of people's trust. The Bible study should not become a place where we seek to vindicate our own unique identities as exceptions to people's prejudices, which will always vary anyway. Nor should we focus too much attention on affirming the people's culture, sexual orientation, gang affiliation, social class, or nationality. Rather, our desire should be to focus people's attention on Jesus. We need to minimize barriers so that people can receive God's living word as it is mediated through us—and in spite of us. Trust will naturally grow among us as we humbly point people away from ourselves and towards Jesus, who is the Savior for us all. We can seek to emulate the attitude of John the Baptist towards Jesus when he says: "He must increase, but I must decrease" (Jn 3:30).

PREPARING TO FACILITATE A GUERRILLA BIBLE STUDY

Before Gathering

Prepare spiritually through personal study, prayer, and worship (as discussed in chapter seven). Spend regular time in God's presence in ways that nourish you, asking the Holy Spirit to fill and refresh you. Ask friends who pray for you to intercede before, during, and after your group Bible studies. Invite the Holy Spirit for prophetic revelation about which

Scriptures to read, questions to ask, and words of knowledge so you can engage personally with participants.

Prayerfully decide how you will order your time so that you can accomplish your objectives, taking into consideration your host's requests, time limit, additional time constraints should interpretation be needed, protocol, the composition of your group, and other considerations. Choose a biblical passage based on these considerations, along with your knowledge of people's needs, their exposure to the Christian faith, and the Spirit's guidance.

Coordinate with your partner or team members, deciding each person's role in advance in order to avoid confusion.

Setting up the Gathering Space

There are unique challenges to facilitating Bible studies, depending on whether you are in someone's home, shelter, work place, hospital room, or street corner. Recommended protocols vary greatly from culture to culture, so it will be important to discern what is respectful for your context. Wherever possible, try to find a meeting place where you can safely read Scripture, minister, and where people will feel free to share their thoughts and feelings with minimal interruptions.

Try to set up the space for optimal participation, arranging chairs or couches in a circle whenever possible. A circle places the facilitator at the same level or below those gathered, creating an environment of equality that puts people at ease. If gathering around a table, space chairs so that participants will be comfortable. Try to leave adequate room behind the chairs to allow for prayer or ministry.

Choose a seat where everyone can easily see and hear you. If you will be accompanied by other ministry workers, encourage them to find seats spaced around the circle. This can help minimize "us-them" dynamics where people's attention is too much on you and your colleagues. In some contexts, people may feel uncomfortable looking at each other and prefer to face in the same direction towards the facilitator.

If speaking to a larger group from a lectern, try to move the lectern to the floor in order to minimize the physical distance between you and your audience. If you are being hosted by another leader, sensitively work out these details in advance.

Whenever possible, place a Bible on every chair before the study begins. Jails and prisons tend to have only the King James Version, which can be hard to understand, so you may want to pass out photocopies of the biblical text in the translation you prefer.

If you will be gathering in someone's home, determine a time and space when there will be minimal interruptions. When you arrive, wait to be invited in and be careful not to look around in ways that could bring shame. Accept whatever seating is offered—even the only or best seats. Some people may be ashamed of their living conditions and ask to gather outside. If televisions or radios are playing, let your hosts to decide whether or not to turn them off.

FACILITATING A GUERRILLA GOSPEL ENCOUNTER

Establish Group Rapport

In jail, prison, or homeless shelter settings, you might want to stand by the door as people enter, shaking their hands, introducing yourself, and inviting them to take a seat. It's important to establish respectful rapport within the group through introductions. When I introduce myself to a new group, I try to provide them with enough information to establish some basic trust. I often begin by verbally acknowledging apparent differences between myself and the group to establish rapport and set people at ease. With prisoners, I may introduce myself with something like the following.

Hey, you guys, I'm Bob, one of the pastors from Tierra Nueva in Burlington. I've been coming into this jail for twenty-four years now and consider it a great privilege to be here with you. I am so sorry that you have to be locked up here in the jail right now. Jails and prisons are hard places, and they certainly aren't working to reform people, are they?

You guys each come from backgrounds that are different from each other's—and certainly from mine. Many of you have suffered in ways that I can't even imagine. You see life and will notice things in the Bible that I may never notice. I've never been arrested or jailed, never crossed over the border illegally, never used heroine or meth, and never been in a fight. Though I've been through my own share of suffering, my life's been very different from yours. So I want to hear what you think and if you notice anything that gives you hope as we read the Bible together.

Invite participation from everyone in the group right at the start, acknowledging that each person brings his or her own unique culture and life perspective, questions, and wisdom. Carefully lay out any necessary ground rules in a gentle, non-legalistic way to provide security for the group. People also appreciate being informed about what you are hoping to accomplish during the time, along with a proposed schedule. Always ask if participants are okay with the plan or if they have other hopes or ideas.

In settings where people already know one another, you might begin with a quick check-in, paying careful attention to how much time you allot to each person so that you can stay within your time limit. In settings where people don't know each other, such as jail, prison, psychiatric hospitals or retirement centers give them clear guidance as to what you're asking them to share, like their first names and where they're from. This humanizes people, especially if they are accustomed to being addressed by their last names or inmate identification numbers.

Use care in making eye contact with people, showing honor and respect according to cultural, gender, and social class considerations. Avoid staring at people, their tattoos, scars, or unique features on their body. I sometimes pray a prayer like this in preparation for being with people: "Jesus, I give you my eyes. May the people experience your tender gaze through me. Help me to see each one as you see them." Seek to acknowledge everyone and avoid showing favoritism or giving too much attention to attention-seeking participants.

Avoid language that over-identifies with people or goes beyond your authentic experience. For example, if you are working with gang-affiliated people but do not come from this background, avoid trying to gain street credibility by using slang that is not part of your normal vocabulary. Also avoid using profanity as this can also discredit you, create offense, or invite unbridled profanity.

Open with Prayer and Worship

When we begin a Bible study with prayer, we recognize our need for God to help us and invite the Spirit to open everyone's hearts. When meeting with people who are not from a religious background, I often explain that when we pray, we are talking to God. I always pray with my eyes open, looking gently over everyone gathered around the circle.

In rural Honduras, where the groups I used to lead included people who didn't attend church, along with active Roman Catholics, Pentecostals, and Baptists, I learned the importance of beginning gatherings with the Lord's Prayer or stating that I or another volunteer would give the opening prayer. Without clear instructions, Pentecostals would break out in simultaneous prayer, often in tongues, alarming the rest of the group. Praying the Lord's Prayer together allowed everyone to participate in an orderly, non-threatening way.

In many settings it helps to silence or bind voices of accusation or mockery or other spirits you discern right at the beginning, either silently or aloud. We can exercise spiritual authority in alignment with Jesus' giving his disciples authority to bind and loose (Mat 16:19; 18:18). I often include in my opening prayer something like this: "In Jesus' name I silence all voices of accusation and mockery, and I welcome the Holy Spirit's presence to bring peace and security." People who are tormented by accusing voices often mention that these voices go dead in response to such declarations—which are not prayers to God but orders directed at predatory invisible realities. I sometimes take some time to explain to people the power of Jesus' name, encouraging them to themselves cry out to Jesus when they feel anxious or tormented.

After the opening prayer, you might consider having a time of singing or silently praying for people around the circle with music before starting the Bible study. In homeless shelters, jails, and prisons, I tend to avoid having people sing together, since not everyone will know the same songs, creating an "us–them" dynamic that can get things off to a bad start. Moreover, songs can trigger negative or positive nostalgia, which can create unnecessary barriers. People may feel pressured by circumstances or remorse to return to the religion of their upbringing, which may have included toxic elements.

In contexts where singing together is appropriate, choose songs that use accessible language and convey the love of God. If possible, it's also a good idea to have photocopied song sheets available.

In contexts where singing together may not be a good idea, most people are receptive to being prayed for while someone plays guitar and sings a contemplative worship song over them. I always ask people's permission, saying something like, "Before we begin, we'd like to play and sing a worship song. Rather than trying to sing along, we invite you to sit back and receive what God wants to give you to bless and refresh you. During the song, I'd like to pray silently over each of you. If you're not comfortable with me praying for you for whatever reason, no worries. Otherwise are you ok with me going around and praying for you?" I ask. I look around from person to person as I'm speaking, and almost always everyone expresses their agreement in some way.

Then I invite the Holy Spirit to bless and comfort us all. I often place my hand gently on the person's shoulder, except when there are no-touch rules or when people express reluctance. In any case I always ask people's permission before even touching them on the shoulder. As I go around the circle, I sometimes feel led to share a prophetic impression about a possible need for physical or emotional healing or to pray specifically for an individual. Once I've gone around the circle, I ask if people need healing for the conditions I've discerned. Then I pray, inviting people to place their hands wherever they need healing on their body. I always make sure I have people's permission before I minister to them in any way.

Prepare to Engage People in Guerrilla Gospel Encounters

I try to remain open about how to begin the Bible study portion of the gathering, based on the Spirit's guidance. Sometimes I give the group options about how to use the remaining time. For example, I might begin with a question or a description of a common problem that people face as a way to get people talking and to prepare them to hear from Scripture. In jails, prisons, or other institutional settings, where people have little control over their schedules, I sometimes ask the group if anyone has a pressing question or Scripture they would like to read and discuss. Or I might begin with a story, testimony, or a prophetic impression for healing or personal encouragement. Sometimes I begin by simply reading the biblical text I've prepared in advance.

Another possibility is to begin with a bibliodrama that enacts the story. Bibliodramas draw from the best practices in improv[127] and psychodrama and can powerfully communicate the gospel and make it accessible to different audiences.[128] Spontaneously gathering volunteers to act out a biblical story can also get people's attention in fresh ways, particularly when combined with a text-based Bible study. I often put together simple bibliodramas, such as Jesus' calling of Simon through the miraculous catch (Lk 5:1–11), the healing of the woman bent over double (Lk 13:10–17),[129] Jesus' encounter with the woman caught in adultery (Jn 4),[130] and the healing of the man who was lame from birth (Acts 3:1–10). To put together a spontaneous bibliodrama, you need to know the biblical story well, be able to think quickly on your feet as you facilitate, and have someone read the story clearly and loudly so that everyone can hear the Scripture as it's being performed.

Engage People in Guerrilla Gospel Encounter

The Bible contains the larger story of God's liberation movement. Within it are many smaller stories situated in many unique settings. Some stories or teachings will appear more immediately relevant to you and your group than others. As you turn to the biblical text, begin by providing a short but compelling reason about why you're inviting people to look at this particular text. This will help participants feel secure and engaged from the start. Also, some people may want to understand why you are reading something from the middle or end of the Bible rather than starting at the beginning, as you would any other book.

127. See Peter Pitzele, *Scripture Windows: Towards a Practice of Bibliodrama* (Los Angeles: Torah Aurora Productions, 1998). For an example of Pitzele's spontaneous bibliodrama, see: https://www.youtube.com/watch?v=omvx96XdnXY. You can also watch the introductory sessions on bibliodrama at: https://www.youtube.com/watch?v=MNPeoKWlSEo and https://www.youtube.com/watch?v=-AbrjNwiXDs

128. See Robin Gallaher Branch, *Six Biblical Plays for Contemporary Audiences* (Eugene: Cascade Books, 2016).

129. See Bob Ekblad, *The Beautiful Gate: Enter Jesus' Global Liberation Movement* (Burlington: The People's Seminary Press, 2017), 76–79.

130. See Ekblad, "Reading Scripture for Good News," 243–249.

Next, briefly outline God's mission in the world in a way that will connect personally with the background and composition of your group. Be sure to use clear, simple language rather than religious jargon or complicated theological vocabulary. When considering how to summarize the Bible to prepare for a particular text, it is wise to determine the key points in advance.

Before turning to an example of what this summary introduction might look like using the story of Jesus' encounter with the blind beggar at the entrance to Jericho (Lk 18:35–43), the following are some important things to keep in mind as you help your group navigate the Bible. For some participants, the biblical narrative might be new or hostile territory.

Navigation Tips

First, in order to keep everyone focused, it's a good idea to read no more than one to three verses of the biblical narrative at a time (based on pre-determined sections of meaning, as discussed in chapter 7). When you read more than three verses of Scripture aloud, people are likely to become distracted and miss some critical content, especially if you are reading in more than one language. Another objective in reading shorter sections of Scripture is to slow down the reading process, inviting contemplation. At the same time, be aware of time limitations and people's attention span and level of engagement, keeping the momentum going to avoid losing people's interest. Holding people's attention is critical in setting the stage for the unfolding biblical narrative.

Second, people who are unfamiliar with the Bible may feel intimidated or embarrassed when they cannot readily find the biblical passage, so show people where to find the passage in the Bible, providing a page number if possible. If people have different versions of the Bible with different page numbers and you see them struggling, gently help individuals find the text. I often try to diffuse any shame from the start by stating that there are many different books in the Bible, and many of them are short and quite difficult to find.

Third, I try to diffuse shame at the beginning of a Bible study by acknowledging that the Bible is foreign and has many words, names, and places that are difficult to pronounce. If a reader has limited reading ability, offer gentle encouragement and help with difficult pronunciation, but don't bother with pronunciation that makes no difference to the meaning (like names of people and places). But the biblical text can spring to life in fresh ways when read slowly or haltingly by an amateur reader.

Fourth, if the same person continually volunteers to read, suggest that someone who hasn't read yet be given the opportunity to read the next verses or to re-read a text that needs closer study. Never pressure anyone to read aloud or offer their opinions

Fifth, only ask questions that have answers anyone in the group could in some way answer. I would never ask someone who the Pharisees or Sadducees are, or what a parable is or why Jewish religious leaders didn't think Jesus should heal on the Sabbath. Questions that require background information can expose people's ignorance, causing them to potentially feel stupid or shamed. I find it best to myself offer the most essential definitions and then ask questions that have answers people can find in the Biblical passage. If I see people hesitating I often invite someone to re-read aloud the verse in question, and then re-ask the question. If a question doesn't bear fruit abandon it and try another. Questions should move the conversation along, helping people determine the meaning of the text and read it in direct rapport with their lives.

Sixth, you may consider dividing a larger group into small groups to discuss the verses, questions, contemporary equivalents or possible responses. Small group discussion works well with students, church groups or people who are accustomed to working together. Identifying or assigning small group facilitators can help assure that everyone has an opportunity to speak and keep the group on track. If your group is made up of inmates, includes people with mental health issues or people under the influence of drugs or alcohol, small group facilitators must be especially skilled. If skilled small group facilitators are not available it is best to keep the larger group together.

Seventh, record people's answers on newsprint paper or a white board if appropriate and possible. It can be empowering for people to see their own answers written down for all to see. Accurately summarizing and recording people's responses requires skill that facilitators unable to spell or write legibly may find intimidating. However this skill can be developed.

Eighth, if you are working with a mixed group (including people from diverse denominations), you may need to use versions considered sacred by each group. If your Bible study is bilingual or trilingual, it is important to have the Scripture read out loud in each of the languages represented within the group, or to have interpreter(s) offer simultaneous translations. If there are a small number of people from a different language group and time is limited, suggest that these individuals read along silently in their language. If possible offer simultaneous interpretation in such cases. This is particularly important for groups that might include participants who are illiterate, or participants who might be able to read but don't have reading glasses (which is common in a jail context).

Finally, if you are using an interpreter, be attentive to the interpreter's skill level, adjusting the speed of your delivery as necessary. Model respectful partnership, occasionally asking both the people and interpreter if everyone is understanding what's being said. Pay attention to those on the edge of the group who may be marginalized, looking for ways to acknowledge and include them. At the break, check with a couple of fluent bilingual people in the group to make sure the interpreter is accurate. If not, find a gentle way to switch to a new one. Ideally, another interpreter should be available so your interpreter can get a break.

Sample Introduction

Following is an example of an introduction that places Jesus' encounter with the blind beggar at the entrance to Jericho (Lk 18:35–43) within the larger story of God.

We're going to read together a story about how Jesus stopped for a blind beggar who was crying out for mercy. Jesus' way of helping him is really surprising. We'll see how the man gets his sight back—but not like you might think. I'm looking forward to hearing how you think this story might bring hope to us here and now. Before we read the story, let's talk about the bigger story of the Bible and what happens before and after the story we're going to read.

The Bible begins by describing how God made humans and gave us a mission. We see God going after humans to recruit them, even when they fail. God calls a couple, Abraham and Sarah, who are caught up in all kinds of troubles, and invites them to leave their homeland and totally trust him. He promises that he'll bless them and multiply them into a great nation. Through their offspring, he says he'll bless every family in the world. Well, this nation, Israel, ends up going through all kinds of ups and downs, choosing to be like all the other nations, appointing corrupt politicians and worshipping false gods—rebelling against God, then returning, then rebelling over and over again.

Israel has one king early on named David, whom God promises will have a descendant who will reign forever and ever. More failures cause many people to give up believing that the promised offspring of Abraham, the son of David, will ever come—but God never forgets his promises, and some people continue to believe. Then Jesus is born, whom Christians believe is the descendant of Abraham, the son of David, God's own son. The second part of the Bible is called the New Testament and tells the story of Jesus' birth, life, death, and resurrection. Luke's Gospel is the third account of this story about Jesus.

The story we're going to read is about Jesus' encounter with a blind man. It happens right before Jesus goes to Jerusalem, where a group of leaders arrest and kill him. Let's see how this blind man trusts in Jesus and how Jesus blesses and recruits him. All four Gospels tell us that Jesus' death isn't the end of the story, for he is resurrected and meets his disciples again—commissioning them to announce salvation and recruit more workers for God's mission of liberation.

Journeying through a Guerrilla Gospel Encounter

Luke 18:35

After introducing the story, I have someone read the first verse: "As Jesus was approaching Jericho, a blind man was sitting by the road begging" (Lk 18:35).

Then I invite the group to identify what's happening in the text. I might ask them to name the characters in the story, where they are located, and what they are doing or saying. For this story, I might ask,

"Who are the characters are and what they are doing?" People observe that Jesus is coming towards Jericho, and a blind man is sitting by the road begging.

In order for the Bible to connect with our lives, we need to envision what the story could look like here and now where we live. As facilitators, we can help this process by asking questions that connect the biblical story to the stories held within the group. Possible questions for this story might include: "Have you ever run into people begging? Why do you think people beg? What would it be like to be blind if there were no welfare system? What situations besides blindness can you identify, which would cause someone to be completely dependent and needy enough to beg?"

Luke 18:37–38

Next, I ask someone to read verses 37–38: "Now hearing a crowd going by, he began to inquire what this was. They told him that Jesus of Nazareth was passing by. And he called out, saying, "Jesus, Son of David, have mercy on me!" (Lk 18:36–38).

Again, I ask who the characters are and what they're doing and saying. Someone says that the blind man hears a crowd going by and asks what's happening—and the crowd tells him that Jesus of Nazareth is passing by. Someone else notices that Jesus must have been famous because the man cries out to him for mercy.

To invite deeper reflection, I ask, "What do you think the blind man was expecting from Jesus when he asked him for mercy?"

Someone else notices that the blind man calls Jesus, "Son of David."

I ask if anyone knows the significance of this title, and if no one responds, I say, "The blind man calls Jesus 'Son of David,' which shows that he sees him as the coming Messiah, who Jewish people were waiting for to liberate Israel from oppressors and bring in paradise."

If there's time and interest I may also mention the prophecy given to David in 2 Samuel 7:11-16 about one of his descendants who will be given an eternal Kingdom. I may even invite people to read Psalms like Psalm 2 and 110 and talk more about what people were expecting this

Messiah to accomplish, or encourage them to check out these Scriptures on their own.

"When this blind man yells out that Jesus is the Son of David, some people might have worried about Roman soldiers overhearing—because it's a revolutionary and subversive title," I mention.

Depending on the context, I might also explain that the word "call out" in Greek (*boaō*) means "to cry or shout with unusually loud volume… 'to scream.'"[131]

Luke 18:39–41

Then I transition into the next verses, saying, "let's see how Jesus responds to this guy."

I ask a new volunteer to read verses 39–41: "Those who led the way were sternly telling him to be quiet; but he kept crying out all the more, 'Son of David, have mercy on me!' And Jesus stopped and commanded that he be brought to him; and when he came near, he questioned him, 'What do you want me to do for you?' And he said, 'Lord, I want to regain my sight!'"

Again, I ask the group to summarize what's happening. If someone says that people tell the blind man to be quiet, I might ask: "Why are they trying to silence him?"

Participants might observe that the people are afraid because he cried out, "Son of David." Then I might say, "I wonder if the crowd considers this man unworthy of Jesus' attention?"

From this place of wondering, I might ask a series of reflective questions, such as, "Are there people whom our society considers unworthy of 'important' people's attention? Do you know anyone who might think of themselves as unworthy of God's attention? Do people today think God is too busy to pay attention to their needs? Has anyone ever tried to silence you or keep people from helping you?"

When it's time to return to the text, I might ask concrete questions about the story, such as, "How does the blind man respond to the crowd's

131. Louw and Nida, *Accordance Version 11.0.3* (November 2014).

efforts to exclude him? What does this tell us about how he sees Jesus? What does the blind man say to Jesus? How does Jesus respond?"

People might notice Jesus' advocacy for the blind beggar by observing that he stops, commands the crowd to bring the man to him, and then asks the man, "What do you want me to do for you?"

Once again, depending on the context, I might inform the group that when the man cries out here, another Greek verb, *krazō,* is used, which means "to call aloud (shriek, exclaim, entreat), cry (out)."[132]

Since one of my objectives in facilitating Bible studies is to help inexperienced readers grow in confidence that they can read the Bible on their own, I might ask a theological question that connects Jesus to God, such as, "If Jesus reveals God, then what do we know about God based on what Jesus does here?"

People might notice that Jesus' actions reveal that God hears, respects, and responds to the cries of a blind beggar, someone who is rejected by the world. Then I might connect these responses to how we see Jesus and God today by asking, "Do you think people see God this way now? How might this understanding change our relationship with God?"

Luke 18:42

Then I transition into this next verse in the story by asking, "Let's listen carefully to what Jesus says and does in this next verse: "And Jesus said to him, "Receive your sight; your faith has made you well."

After another volunteer reads the text, I might ask a question about what people see. "Does Jesus do anything? What does he say? What happens here?"

Bible study participants sometimes offer responses that they think will please the facilitator or support what they think is the orthodox viewpoint. If someone responds to these questions by saying, "Jesus healed the blind man," I would affirm what is true in the statement and then ask questions to invite closer analysis. "Yes, we can see that the man regains his sight. But let's try to look more closely at how it actually happens.

132. Key dictionary of Greek, *Accordance Version 11.0.3*, November 2014.

What does Jesus say exactly?" Then I might ask someone else to re-read Luke 18:42.

When you invite people to read more closely, they will often speak out more exact responses. "Jesus tells the blind man to receive his sight," someone might say. Rarely will someone say what is also fairly obvious—that Jesus deflects attention from what he does "for" the blind man, even though he's asked him, "what do you want me to do for you?"

Sometimes we need to challenge people's thinking by risking a provocative interpretation. Here, Jesus empowers the blind man, inviting him to receive his sight. I want people to get this idea, which is confirmed when Jesus gives the blind man all the credit for the healing: "*your faith* has made you well." You may need to offer these insights, since they directly challenge dominant theological views that identify Jesus as the primary agent and the blind man as a passive beneficiary.

I might follow these observations with another question, such as, "where do we see the blind man's faith?" Some people might mention the blind man crying out for mercy to Jesus, or his bold response: "Lord, I want to regain my sight!" Others might recognize his willingness to receive his sight.

Luke 18:43

Again, I ask people to pay attention to what happens in this final verse in the story and then invite a volunteer to read verse 43: "Immediately he regained his sight and began following Him, glorifying God; and when all the people saw it, they gave praise to God."

People easily identify the final actions: the man's immediate recovery of sight, his following of Jesus, and his glorifying of God. One important observation to make is that all the people who were walking along with Jesus see the healing and praise God.

In a final summary, I might return to a theological question about what this verse reveals about God, since one of the primary objectives of a Bible study is to strengthen people's faith and trust in God as good and loving. I might ask, "Why are all the people glorifying him here?" I might go on to reflect on the way that the people who normally exclude this blind beggar now see that he is publicly valued, miraculously healed, honored before everyone for his faith, and is a worshipful recruit of Jesus.

Respond to the Journey: Watch, Pray, Minister

As I continue to watch and pray for ways to invite people into the story, I ask people to think about what they would say if Jesus asked, "What do you want me to do for you?" I say that I believe that Jesus is alive now, and that we can cry out for mercy like the blind man. Then I reflect on the fact that Jesus required faith from the blind man, since he was asking for a miracle.

Then I suggest that we take some time to think about what we would ask for from Jesus. I acknowledge that this might be difficult and suggest that we pray, asking the Holy Spirit to guide our longings. After a moment of silence, I invite people to share, affirming that it's totally fine for people to keep this to themselves. Then I invite people to name their requests silently before Jesus. While they think and pray, I ask Jesus what he wants to do for the people in the group.

During this time of prayerful response, it's important to listen and look for prophetic revelation based on what you hear God saying, people's responses, and the direction of the Spirit. Pay close attention to what you are noticing in the group, on the screen of your imagination, and in any spontaneous thoughts that arise (see chapter 5 for more about this). Ask Jesus to show you what he wants you to notice and what he wants to do for people while they are thinking and praying.

Quickly evaluate any impressions to which you think you need to respond, either for individuals or the group. If you discern you're to share a prophetic impression to encourage, challenge or pray for healing, ask each person's permission before sharing your impression or humbly offering your word.

When I feel led to invite people to choose to follow or surrender to Jesus, I ask everyone to stand in a circle and suggest that anyone who feels drawn towards Jesus can take a step forward as a way of imagining themselves moving closer to him. When people physically respond, I invite them to speak out directly to Jesus about their desire to surrender their lives. Then I lead them in a simple prayer. When inviting people to receive the Holy Spirit or the peace of Christ, I suggest that they put out their hands or open their palms as if receiving a gift. People who are desperate may doubt their motivations or prefer to keep their decision private to avoid mockery, so I also make space for people to do these gestures secretly, expressing their desire directly to God.

If time permits, I ask if anyone has additional prayer requests and then pray accordingly, or I invite people to share their requests as prayers. If there's still time, I wrap up by inviting people to share what they'll be taking away from our time together. If most people are familiar with the Lord's Prayer, I often close our time by praying it together.

Facilitating liberating Bible studies can be an adventurous journey leading to many positive outcomes. When we look at how Jesus engaged people during his earthly ministry we see him moving in freedom, wisdom and in power, combining teaching with signs and wonders that confirmed his words. In our next and final chapter we will explore diverse manifestations of the Spirit, familiarizing ourselves with an arsenal available to all who seek to follow Jesus in his dangerous but life-giving movement to announce and embody the Kingdom of God.

CHAPTER NINE

GUERRILLA TACTICS: SIGNS, WONDERS, JUSTICE & MERCY

Jesus and the apostles often combine the proclamation of the word, gifts of the Spirit, and acts of justice and mercy to demonstrate the love of God. As ministry practitioners imitating the way of Jesus, we are called to announce the Kingdom of God as well by teaching and declaring good news to the unreached and by demonstrating Jesus' victory over the powers with miraculous signs, which include acts of justice and mercy, physical and emotional healing, deliverance, and more. These signs are essential guerrilla tactics, providing immediate on-the-ground training that gives people a foretaste of the Kingdom of God and propels them to join Jesus' movement.

Through dialogical Bible studies, both facilitators and participants can witness and experience the resurrected Jesus drawing near. Mark's Gospel ends with a clear affirmation of the dynamic, visible ways that Jesus will continue to work with us: "So then, when the Lord Jesus had spoken to them, He was received up into heaven and sat down at the right hand of God. And they went out and preached everywhere, while the Lord worked with them, and confirmed the word by the signs that followed" (16:19–20).

I regularly witness signs that seem to confirm the word. As Bible study participants experience physical and emotional healing, freedom from demonic oppression, as well as family, legal, or financial breakthroughs, we witness signs that confirm Mark's description of the resurrected Jesus accompanying us and working alongside us. Since life involves ongoing struggle in the midst of hostile powers, we need to keep asking, seeking, and waiting in expectation for the Kingdom to continue to advance as Jesus confirms our proclamations with miraculous signs and wonders.

The Gospels and the book of Acts present us with a vast array of signs, wonders, and actions that accompany the vocal proclamation of the good news of the Kingdom of God. When Jesus is teaching and preaching in the cities, the disciples of John the Baptist approach him to ask if he is the Messiah. His response clearly identifies the signs of God's Kingdom: "'Go and report to John what you hear and see. The blind receive sight and the lame walk, the lepers are cleansed and the deaf hear, the dead are raised up, and the poor have the gospel preached to them'" (Mt 11:5).

Many of Jesus' actions function as signs, and some fulfill Old Testament prophecies of the coming Messiah. Jesus directs fishermen to let down their nets for miraculous catches of fish (Lk 5:4; Jn 21:6); he multiplies loaves and fish to feed crowds (Mk 6:41-43); he walks on water (Mk 6:48-49); he drives out moneychangers from the temple (Mt 21:12); he advocates for the tax collectors and sinners (Mk 2:16-17); he drives a legion of demons our of a tormented man into a herd of pigs that consequently rush over a cliff into the sea (Lk 8:33). Jesus heals on the Sabbath (Jn 9:14) and touches the unclean in direct defiance of religious authorities. He is rejected by the Jewish leaders of Israel, dies between two criminals, and is raised from the dead on the third day. Jesus' words are constantly confirmed by actions and miraculous signs with personal and social implications. Our own reading of Scripture should inspire our imaginations and expectations for now—and also for later.

In John's Gospel, there are seven specific events identified as signs,[133] which include: the changing of water to wine (Jn 2:1–11), the healing from a distance of the royal official's son in Capernaum (Jn 4:46–54), the healing of the paralytic at Bethesda (Jn 5:1–15), the multiplication of loaves to feed five thousand (Jn 6:5–14), the healing of the man blind

133. Some scholars include Jesus' walking on the water in Jn 6:15–24 and the miraculous catch of fish in Jn 21:1–14. See John Hutchison, *Our Lord's Signs in St. John's Gospel: Discussions Chiefly Exegetical and Doctrinal on the Eight Miracles in the Fourth Gospel,* (Edinburgh, 1892).

from birth (Jn 9:1–7), the raising of Lazarus from the dead (Jn 12:18), and Jesus' death on the cross and resurrection (Jn 19–20). What might these signs look like today? John states clearly the purpose of sharing these signs at the end of his Gospel: "Therefore many other signs Jesus also performed in the presence of the disciples, which are not written in this book; but these have been written so that you may believe that Jesus is the Christ, the Son of God; and that believing you may have life in his name" (Jn 20:30–31).

The signs Jesus performed often inspired belief in him and can continue to do so today (see Jn 2:23; 3:2; 6:2, 14; 7:23). Belief leads to trust as we follow Jesus each day, but lack of belief leads to spiritual death. Sometimes Jesus' signs do not inspire belief (Lk 11:29; Jn 12:37), and sometimes the signs attract interest that Jesus critiques (Jn 4:48; 6:26). Jesus also warns his followers of pretenders who will perform false signs and wonders in order to lead people astray (Mk 13:22). Thus there's always a need for vigilance, yet not for cynicism.

Peter draws attention to signs during Jesus' earthly ministry: "Men of Israel, listen to these words: Jesus the Nazarene, a man attested to you by God with miracles and wonders and signs which God performed through Him in your midst, as you yourselves know" (Acts 2:22). Certain signs are performed by Jesus' disciples as a continuation of his earthly ministry: "These signs will accompany those who have believed: in my name they will cast out demons, they will speak with new tongues" (Mk 16:17). In these stories and in the Apostle Paul's writings, we see the first apostles being given manifestations of the Spirit. The manifestations of the Spirit are concrete happenings that benefit people in distinct ways. In the next section, we'll look briefly at the various manifestations of the Spirit mentioned in these writings to see how they might further support our ministry. First, a brief introduction will set the manifestations of the Spirit within the larger context of Jesus' liberation movement.

MANIFESTATIONS OF THE SPIRIT

In the Apostle Paul's first epistle to the Corinthians, he identifies three distinct categories of guerrilla tactics in the Spirit's arsenal, which are available to all Jesus followers: "gifts" (*charisma*), "ministries" (*diakonia*), and "effects" (*energema*). "Effects" are acts, deeds, operations, or workings, which Paul emphasizes have their source in God—the supreme strategist and master of the universe: "There are varieties of effects (*energema*), but the same God who works (*energeo*) all things in all persons" (1 Cor 12:6). Paul describes all of these categories as "manifestations of the Spirit for the common good" (v. 7). In order to communicate God's love effectively and to inspire others to join Jesus, we need to understand these distinct categories and how they each function.

Gifts of the Spirit

When seeking to communicate spiritual truths with not-yet-believing people in foreign or potentially hostile settings, there are no maps or ready-made techniques that will guarantee success. It often feels like bushwhacking through the wilderness or maneuvering through minefields or booby-trapped terrain behind enemy lines. The Spirit provides guidance, special revelation, and even miracles that can help us survive and move forward. In Paul's earliest list of the arsenal of gifts, he identifies word of wisdom, word of knowledge, faith, healing, effecting of miracles, prophesy, distinguishing of spirits, various kinds of tongues, and interpretation of tongues (1 Cor 12:8–10). Later, near the end of Paul's life, he adds gifts that broaden the possibilities for redemptive action in the world: teaching, exhorting, giving, leading, and showing mercy (Rom 12:6–8).[134] Following is an exploration of how some of these manifestations of the Spirit can confirm the word during guerrilla Bible studies.

Word of Wisdom

Paul identifies "the word of wisdom" as the first God-given manifestation of the Spirit, which suggests its high value in communicating good news (1 Cor 12:8). It is paired with "word of knowledge," a closely related

134. Gordon D. Fee, *God's Empowering Presence: The Holy Spirit in the Letters of Paul* (Grand Rapids: Baker Academic, 1994), 164–175; Mark Stibbe, *Know Your Spiritual Gifts: How to Minister in the Power of the Spirit* (Grand Rapids: Zondervan, 1997).

gift enabling communication.[135] The Greek noun *logos* (word) that is used in the expressions "word of wisdom" (*logos sophias*) and "word of knowledge" (*logos gnosis*) is best translated as "message" or "utterance," suggesting inspired revelatory speech.

The effective transmission of life-giving gospel truths to not yet reached people groups in new settings requires precise revelations and articulate and sometimes unprecedented communications. Utterances of wisdom and knowledge can appear when we feel lost or in a perilous state—arriving as communications of divine intelligence that can inform our overall strategy or enable effective combat. These divine communications can function as life-giving ordnance from above— powerful and effective at removing barriers.

Yet they appear less as certainties and more as unassuming thoughts that must be spoken if they're to be released—like pulling a pin out of a grenade so it will detonate. Revelations must be spoken out loud in order to bring immediate and lasting relief. The revelations may come in a stream of successive thoughts that must be spoken one after another, bringing understanding that challenges and replaces fortresses of mind and spirit. Revelations may emerge spontaneously through Bible study participants as they share. However they emerge, these revelations facilitate life-changing encounters between people and God.

"Utterance of wisdom" seems to refer specifically to spoken revelation about the mystery of *how* God saves us through Christ Jesus.[136] Paul makes this connection when he writes that the preaching of Christ crucified is "the power of God and the wisdom of God" (1 Cor 1:23–24), that saves "those who believe" (1 Cor 1:21). Yet belief needs to be inspired by the revelation of this wisdom, which is "not of this age nor of the rulers of this age, who are passing away" (1 Cor 2:6). Paul emphasizes that divine wisdom is hidden, inaccessible to the rulers of this age, "for if they had understood it they would not have crucified the Lord of glory" (1 Cor

135. This first pair is followed by other pairs: "gifts of healing . . . and . . . effecting of miracles," "prophesy . . . and . . . discernment of spirits," and "various kinds of tongues . . . and interpretation of tongues" (vv. 9–10). See Stibbe, *Know Your Spiritual Gifts*, 47 and Fee, *God's Empowering Presence*, 167.

136. In *God's Empowering Presence,* Gordon Fee writes, "it is the recognition that the message of Christ crucified is God's true wisdom" (166).

2:8). This hidden wisdom is a secret weapon for Christian combatants, and to access it, we need to be able to recognize when God is speaking.

A word of wisdom often comes as a special insight into a verse or story that reveals Jesus' unique way of being Messiah. In a recent Bible study on Luke 12:35–38 with a group of male prisoners, I began by reading verses 35–36: "Be dressed in readiness, and keep your lamps lit. Be like men who are waiting for their master when he returns from the wedding feast, so that they may immediately open the door to him when he comes and knocks." We tried talking about how they might ready themselves if they were slaves of someone coming back from a wedding—but it's such a foreign scenario that it was much easier to discuss how they'd ready themselves if they knew the guard was coming to knock on their cell door to move them to court, another cellblock, or to a transport van to take them to prison. The men described feeling powerless before someone with greater authority. The men assumed that this text was leading to a familiar version of Christian faith—that it's important to be ready to serve a powerful God whenever you're called, or to be acceptable in case Jesus returns so you'll be taken and not left behind.

Yet as we carefully read and reflected on the next verse, some surprising revelation came: "Blessed are those slaves whom the master will find on the alert when he comes; truly I say to you, that he will gird himself to serve, and have them recline at the table, and will come up and wait on them" (Lk 10:37).

After defining "gird" as "dress," I invited the men to re-read the verse and then describe in their own words what the master will do for those who open the door.

"He comes in to serve them a meal!" someone said.

"If your boss or a guard here at the jail came to your door and knocked, and you opened the door, and then the guard came in to serve you a meal, would you be surprised?" I asked.

"Yes!" they replied. "And it wouldn't happen," someone stated matter of factly. Then we talked about how in this parable, Jesus really challenges people's understanding of God and of Jesus himself. I shared how in the Gospel of Matthew, Jesus says of himself: "the Son of Man did not come to be served, but to serve, and to give his life a ransom for many" (Mt 20:28).

The idea that Jesus pursues us, like someone knocking on our door to come closer to us and humbly serve us, is completely new for people who are used to thinking of God as a distant ruler or law enforcer. Even more surprising is that Jesus gives his life as a ransom, posting himself as bail so we can be free! Yet when I'm sitting at a table with them in jail, this message becomes more believable.

Guiding the men back to the beginning of the passage, where Jesus talks about being ready with a lamp lit for his return, I asked the men, "If we know that Jesus is coming to draw closer to us and serve us, does that make you want to be on the lookout for him?"

Some of the men stated their desire to be on the lookout for Jesus openly, while others communicated with nods. Still other men looked at me like they'd like to believe this could be true but they're afraid to hope and then get disappointed.

Then I shared how at the end of the Bible, Jesus says: "Behold, I stand at the door and knock; if anyone hears my voice and opens the door, I will come in to him and will dine with him, and he with me" (Rev 3:20).

"How might we know when Jesus is knocking on our door?" I asked. "What might it look like to actually open the door and let him in?"

Though people weren't sure, they openly stated their need for and attraction to Jesus and their desire to let him into their lives.

We closed our time together by reading the final verse: "Whether he comes in the second watch, or even in the third, and finds them so, blessed are those slaves" (Lk 10:38). I invited the men to pray with me, that we would hear his knock, recognize his presence, and welcome him in.

The word of wisdom is manifest whenever we believe in, look out for, recognize, and welcome Jesus as a self-emptying, pursuing, and serving master. As Paul writes, this word enables us to perceive, "Things which eye has not seen and ear has not heard, and which have not entered the heart of man, all that God has prepared for those who love him. For to us God revealed them through the Spirit; for the Spirit searches all things, even the depths of God" (1 Cor 2:9–10).

Jesus' means of saving the world as God's son and Israel's Messiah reflects this superior wisdom, which is not of this world. In Christ, God emptied himself, taking on the form of slave, being made in the likeness of a human, he humbled himself by becoming obedient to the point of death on a cross (Phil 2:5–8). God himself reveals this divine wisdom, opening disciples' eyes just as the resurrected Jesus opened Cleopas's and his companion's eyes after explaining the Scriptures to them on the road to Emmaus (Lk 24:31). The Spirit is still available now to enable us to see how Moses, the Prophets, and other Scriptures bear witness to how Christ was to suffer. When revelation happens, we can experience what these early disciples said after Jesus vanished from their sight: "Were not our hearts burning within us while He was speaking to us on the road, while He was explaining the Scriptures to us?" (Lk 24:32).

The epistle of James differentiates divine wisdom from the wisdom of this world:

> Who among you is wise and understanding? Let him show by his good behavior his deeds in the gentleness of wisdom. But if you have bitter jealousy and selfish ambition in your heart, do not be arrogant and so lie against the truth. This wisdom is not that which comes down from above, but is earthly, natural, demonic. For where jealousy and selfish ambition exist, there is disorder and every evil thing. But the wisdom from above is first pure, then peaceable, gentle, reasonable, full of mercy and good fruits, unwavering, without hypocrisy. And the seed whose fruit is righteousness is sown in peace by those who make peace. (3:13–18)

When we share messages of "wisdom from above," we are sowing in peace and will see fruits of righteousness and justice.[137]

Word of Knowledge

A word of knowledge is God-inspired speech that clarifies meaning, helping people know and understand God. This differs from traditional

137. The Greek term δικαιοσύνη (*dikaiosune*) means "to cause someone to be in a proper or right relation with someone else," including with God (Rom 3:24), and all relationships (Rom 9:29; Acts 17:31; 2 Pet 3:13). *Dikaiosune* includes the notion of righteousness and justice, which are unfortunately often seen as completely separate categories in English.

Pentecostal and charismatic understandings of a word of knowledge as revealed information about people's lives, communities, or countries—which fits more in the category of prophesy. As Mark Stibbe writes, "The word of knowledge is an insight into God's thoughts, not ours!"[138] Paul describes this gift as Spirit-revealed knowledge about God:

> The thoughts of God no one knows except the Spirit of God. Now we have received, not the spirit of the world, but the Spirit who is from God, so that we may know[139] the things freely given to us by God, which things we also speak, not in words taught by human wisdom, but in those taught by the Spirit, combining spiritual thoughts with spiritual words. (1 Cor 2:11–13)

Words or utterances of knowledge are those things "taught by the Spirit," as Mark Stibbe states in the following definition: "Word of knowledge is a special anointing in which a believer is given an insight into the unfathomable depths of God's grace—and insight which he or she then articulates in words taught by the Holy Spirit."[140] Stibbe also helpfully articulates the differences between and the complementarities of a word of wisdom and a word of knowledge: "Wisdom is associated with 'how' and knowledge with 'what'. In the light of this, it may therefore be right to infer that theological knowledge refers to insights into God's grace, while theological wisdom refers to insights concerning the way that grace is worked out, particularly in the cross."[141]

Jesus clearly exercised all of these gifts during his life on earth, and we are invited to exercise them, too. The Gospels note that Jesus' listeners were often struck by his wisdom and authority. As a young boy, Jesus stayed behind in Jerusalem to discuss with the teachers in the temple, and "all who heard Him were amazed at his understanding and his answers" (Lk 2:47). People who heard Jesus teach in the synagogue in Capernaum said: "What is this? A new teaching with authority! He

138. Stibbe, *Know Your Spiritual Gifts*, 38.

139. "The Greek verb translated as "know" or "understand" is *eidon*, which is a synonym for *ginoskein*—the verb form of the word *gnosis*, which is used in the word of "knowledge." Mark Stibbe, *Know Your Spiritual Gifts*, 40.

140. Stibbe, *Know Your Spiritual Gifts*, 41.

141. Stibbe, *Know Your Spiritual Gifts*, 47.

commands even the unclean spirits, and they obey him" (Mk 1:22).[142] When he spoke in his hometown synagogue, people said: "Where did this man get this wisdom and these miraculous powers?" (Mt 13:54; Mk 6:2). Later, in the book of Acts, when theologians argued with Stephen, "they were unable to cope with the wisdom and the Spirit with which he was speaking" (Acts 6:10). The Apostle Paul's theology articulates unprecedented mysteries of the Gospel to Jews and Gentiles alike. His revelations fit within the category of "utterance of wisdom and knowledge," as when he states:

> that by revelation there was made known to me the mystery, as I wrote before in brief. By referring to this, when you read you can understand my insight into the mystery of Christ, which in other generations was not made known to the sons of men, as it has now been revealed to His holy apostles and prophets in the Spirit. (Eph 3:3–5)

As we lead Bible studies and engage in discussions about spiritual concerns, we should recognize our need for revelation and anticipate moments of inspiration. When you find yourself communicating specific messages to particular individuals or groups with special clarity, recognize that you are speaking under the inspiration of the Holy Spirit. Pray for revelatory moments for yourself and others—without which people may not be able to receive the message of the Gospel.

In jail or prison Bible studies, I often experience and witness a word of wisdom and word of knowledge manifesting within myself and others. Suddenly a special clarity will come as someone shares, which seems to break through barriers, bringing excitement as people feel the Scriptures speaking directly to them. Once, a young Salvadoran gang member in our Spanish Bible study began re-telling the Bible story using raw, street Spanish. His unique interpretations, examples, and wording were so hilarious and inspired that they dismantled people's defenses, breaking down walls of separation with the invisible power of spiritual revelation.

142. See also Mk 3:5; Lk 4:32, 36.

Faith

Faith is another manifestation of the Spirit that confirms the proclamation of the word. When speaking about faith, we must distinguish between the faith of the one ministering and the faith of the beneficiary. Jesus exercises faith when he orders lepers to go and show themselves to the priests (Lk 17:14), a paralyzed man to take up his pallet and walk (Mk 2:11-12), the dead and buried Lazarus to come out of the tomb (Jn 11:43), and many other miracles. Imagine if we had the faith to speak out healing and new life as he did!

Those whom Jesus heals are often commended for their faith. When the woman with a chronic blood flow touches Jesus in a crowd and is instantly healed, Jesus gives her the credit: "Daughter, your faith has made you well; go in peace and be healed of your affliction" (Mk 5:34). The blind man at the entrance to Jericho responds to Jesus' question, "what do you want me to do for you?" with a faith-filled response: "I want to regain my sight" (Lk 18:41). Though this is an impossible prospect, Jesus says, "Receive your sight; your faith has made you well" (v. 42).

In other stories, both Jesus and the one seeking him have the gift of faith. When the Roman centurion begs Jesus to heal his servant, Jesus is willing, but then the centurion tells him that he's not worthy for Jesus to enter his house (Mt 8:8). "'Just say the word and my servant will be healed,'" he tells Jesus. Jesus commends him for his faith: "'Truly I say to you, I have not found such great faith with anyone in Israel'" (v. 10). Jesus demonstrates his own faith by saying, "'Go; it shall be done for you as you have believed.' And the servant was healed that very moment" (Mt 8:13).

When faith comes upon us, or upon someone to whom we are ministering, the Kingdom of God suddenly draws near. I once led a Bible study with a group of men in the Skagit County Jail on Luke 13:10–17, when Jesus lays his hands on a woman bent over double for eighteen years due to a spirit and heals her, saying, "woman you are freed from you sickness" (v. 12).

When I asked the men how they wanted to respond to the story, a man in his early thirties with a chronic tick that caused him to wince dramatically about every thirty seconds said that he'd like prayer for healing from this tick, which had afflicted him since childhood. I had known this man and observed the tick for many years. Though I had little to no faith for his healing, I agreed to pray for him because of his faith. While praying, I thought that I should ask him if his father had beat him in the head when he was a child.

"All the time," he said, looking at me in surprise. I invited him to consider giving his father a gift that he quite likely didn't deserve—forgiveness! I was surprised when the man said he wanted to forgive his father. Then I led him in a prayer, which included a detailed account of the offenses he was forgiving. The man cried as he described his father's abuse, then forgave and blessed his father. This led to immediate relief of the nervous tick, though it returned several weeks later when his father refused to post bail. As this man continued to forgive his father, he experienced renewed healing from the tick, and his process of reconciliation with his father has continued.

Gifts of Healing

Gifts of healing, which appear to be related to the gift of faith, are practiced by Jesus and the Apostles on nearly every page of the Gospels and Acts of the Apostles,[143] almost always in the context of teaching or preaching. The Gospel of Matthew summarizes Jesus' ministry throughout Galilee as follows:

> Jesus was going throughout all Galilee, teaching in their synagogues and proclaiming the gospel of the kingdom, and healing every kind of disease and every kind of sickness among the people. The news about Him spread throughout all Syria; and they brought to Him all who were ill, those suffering with various diseases and pains, demoniacs, epileptics, paralytics; and He healed them. (Mt 4:23–24)

Jesus healed people in their homes (Mk 1:29–34; 5:35–43), on the beach (Mk 3:7–12; 6:53–56), along the road (Mk 5:24–34; 10:46–52), on

143. The Greek term used here, *charismata iamaton,* "gifts of healing," includes the term *iama* (cure, healing). This term occurs only in 1 Cor 12:9, 28, 30 in the NT. However, the verb *iaomai* (to cure, heal, make whole) occurs often in the Gospels and Acts (Mt 8:8, 13; 13:5; 15:28, 29; Lk 5:17; 6:18; 7:7; 8:46; 9:2, 11, 42; 14:4; Acts 9:34; 10:38; 28:8, 27; Heb 12:13; Jam 5:6; 1 Pet 2:24).

a mountain (Mt 15:29-31), in synagogues (Mk 3:1–6; Lk 13:10–17), in the temple (Mt 21:14), and in towns and cities (Lk 5:12–15; 7:2–17).

Though Jesus often takes the initiative in healing people, he also responds to people's requests. He models the healing of those afflicted by specific physical conditions (blindness, epilepsy, paralysis, chronic bleeding), and "every kind of disease and every kind of sickness" [Mt 9:35]), as well as spiritual affliction from demonic spirits. He gives direct orders, saying: "be opened!" to a deaf mute's ears (Mk 7:34), "be cleansed!" to a leper (Mt 8:3), and "be quiet and come out of him!" to a demon (Mk 1:25). Jesus also heals people by directly touching them and speaking a word, as when he heals two blind men who follow him on the road: "Then He touched their eyes, saying, 'Be it done to you according to your faith'" (Mt 9:29).

Jesus often engages people's faith by empowering them. To a paralytic, he says, "'rise, take up your bed, and go home.' And he rose, and went home," (Mt 9:6–7). To ten lepers, he says, "'Go and show yourselves to the priests.' And as they were going, they were cleansed" (Lk 17:14). To a man born blind, he says, "'Go, wash in the pool of Siloam.' . . . And so he went away and washed, and came back seeing" (Jn 9:7). Jesus also invites people to receive their healing and affirms their faith in the process, such as when he tells the blind beggar, "receive your sight; your faith has made you well" (Lk 18:42).

People often feel unworthy of healing because they see their suffering as a direct consequence of their own destructive choices. Yet throughout the Gospels, Jesus graciously heals people whom the society views as meriting their conditions.[144] When individuals who are suffering from Hepatitis B or C, heroin withdrawal, sexually transmitted diseases, HIV/Aids, diabetes, stabbing or gunshot wounds, or accidents where they are at fault encounter these stories, they can be liberated to seek and receive healing from Jesus. I have seen people healed of lung conditions due to smoking cigarettes or marijuana and of Hepatitis C due to intravenous

144. Sickness was viewed as God's punishment in the OT and amongst Jewish people in the first century. Many of Jesus' healings can be viewed as acts of mercy or even clemency, where sanctions are lifted by as a sign of God's unconditional grace (see Mk 3:1–6; 5:1–19; Lk 5:17–26; Jn 9:1–12).

drug use. On several occasions, I have seen the healing of hands broken from fist fights, from struggles with law-enforcement when resisting arrest, or from inmates striking the cinder-block walls of their cells. These healings confirm the good news that Jesus loves undeserving sinners.

Healing or deliverance from evil spirits often requires people to forgive their enemies and also themselves. As a Bible study leader, you may need to invite people to confess their sins and turn away from particular attitudes linked to their condition. While praying for a young youth worker with chronic, debilitating back pain, the word "reckless" kept coming to mind. I asked if the word "reckless" meant anything to him, and he said that the word described him exactly, and his back pain was due to a motorcycle accident he'd had while riding recklessly. I asked if he had ever confessed his recklessness or carelessness and asked God for forgiveness. He said he never had, but that he wanted to do so. I led him in a prayer of confession and declared his sins forgiven in Jesus' name. I invited him to receive his forgiveness and then to forgive himself for the accident that caused his back pain. As he did this, he was touched by the Holy Spirit and completely healed.

Jesus deputized his new recruits soon after they began following him. He "gave them authority over unclean spirits, to cast them out, and to heal every kind of disease and every kind of sickness" (Mt 10:1).[145] Then he sent them out, saying, "as you go, preach, saying, 'The kingdom of heaven is at hand.' Heal the sick, raise the dead, cleanse the lepers, cast out demons; freely you received, freely give" (Mt 10:7–8).

Effecting of Miracles

In the Spirit's arsenal of gifts identified by Paul in 1 Corinthians 12, the effecting of miracles is named after the gifts of faith and healing in this closely linked triad of related gifts.[146] The Greek, *energemata dunameon,* is translated literally as "workings of powers."[147] "Workings" refers to God's works, as in Galatians 3:5: "So then, does he who provides you with the Spirit and works miracles among you, do it by the works of the

145. See also Lk 9:1; 10:9.

146. Stibbe, *Know Your Spiritual Gifts*, 92.

147. Stibbe, *Know Your Spiritual Gifts,* 92.

law, or by hearing with faith?"[148] So how might we come to practice this gift of effecting miracles during Bible studies or preaching?

For many years I assumed that healings and the effecting of miracles required confidence and a strong and powerful faith. However, in 1 Corinthians 2:3–5, Paul describes his ministry in ways that associate power with weakness:

> I was with you in weakness and in fear and in much trembling, and my message and my preaching were not in persuasive words of wisdom, but in demonstration of the Spirit and of power, so that your faith would not rest on the wisdom of men, but on the power of God.

Years ago, during one of my Thursday evening Bible studies in the Skagit County Jail, I witnessed the "effecting" of a miracle. After some thirty inmates bustled into the jail's multipurpose room, the guards shut the doors and locked us in.[149] Once seated on chairs in a large circle, I invited the men to pray with me for God to send the Holy Spirit to illuminate our reading and discussion. From the start, I noticed an uneasy tension in the room. After invoking the Holy Spirit in prayer, I invited a volunteer to read John 4:1–15, the story of Jesus and the Samaritan woman at the well.

During the reading, I found myself distracted by people's nervous glances and aggressive glares. Several men talked to each other in hushed voices. Pukie, a Mexican gang member in his early twenties with a shoulder bandaged from a gunshot wound he had received while robbing a drug dealer, looked especially agitated. Stimy, a heavily tattooed young white guy doing six years in prison for a drive-by shooting, sat sullenly in between the men on my left.

Looking directly at those who were talking or glaring, I asked, "Who are the participants in this story?" When nobody answered, I invited

148. See also 1 Cor 12:6, 11; Gal 5:6; Eph 3:20; Phil 2:13; Col 1:29; 1 Thes 2:13.

149. This story was originally published in Bob Ekblad, "Jesus' Surprising Offer of Living Cocaine: Contextual encounters at the well with Latino inmates in U.S. jails," in *Through the Eyes of Another: Intercultural Reading of the Bible*, ed. Hans de Wit, Louis Jonker, Marleen Kool, Daniel Schipani (Amsterdam: Vrije Universiteit, 2004), 133–136.

Pukie, the most agitated in the group, to reread John 4:4–8. Then I asked the men to identify the story's characters. After getting feeble responses, I asked Stimy, "So where are they and what's happening in this story?"

"Shit, I don't know man, I wasn't paying attention," Stimy said, looking down at his Bible. "At some well, I guess, talking and shit."

Knowing that many of the men in the group were longtime drug dealers and/or addicts, and grasping for a contemporary equivalent to the well, I invited them to imagine that they were selling drugs out of their apartment. From conversations with hundreds of addicts, I knew how desperate they were to acquire more crack cocaine, which often propelled them into selling drugs to assure their own supply.

"So there you are, and Jesus comes up to your door, but you don't know who he is. He just looks like some normal *gabacho* (white guy), maybe like me. He says, 'hey, sell me some coke,' or 'sell me some crack.'"

The men all look at me, some smiling uneasily, others clearly waiting to hear what I am going to say next. "You wonder if you can trust him, and inside, you are thinking this is an undercover officer trying to make a sting operation. You say to him, 'No way man, I can't help you,' and wish he'd go away. But he keeps talking with you.

"'Hey, listen,' he tells you. 'If you knew God's gift, and if you knew who it is who is asking you to sell him some cocaine, you'd ask him, and he would give you living crack. Because the crack that you smoke only gives you a high for a moment, and you have to keep buying more, but the coke that I will give you will give you a permanent high.'"

Many of the men raised their eyebrows and seemed surprised, even shocked. Then I suggested that this story shows us how Jesus comes to us where we are and respects us. Many of the men kept fidgeting nervously, glancing across the circle, then down at the floor.

Willie, a Chicano man loosely affiliated with gangs who was sitting beside me, tapped me on the shoulder. "We need to wrap this up, Roberto," he told me with urgency in his voice. "Now."

I told the men that it appeared we were all having a hard time focusing and that maybe we should end our study early. I invited them to stand and pray the Lord's Prayer together in Spanish.

Everyone stood, and I closed my eyes and began the prayer. Right away, I could hear that only a few people were praying with me, and I noticed increasing rustling around me. I sped up my prayer and raced for the closing, "deliver us from evil"—the official ending of the Roman Catholic Spanish version of the prayer. Then I opened my eyes.

The men on my left all had their blue chairs raised above their heads, the metal legs ready to crash down upon the men on my right, whose chairs were also raised. A Native American man stood with a leaded microphone jack raised above his head like a tomahawk, ready to come down on Willie's head. I walked quickly through the middle of the crowd to the buzzer on the wall to call the guards. Almost instantly, they arrived on the scene and hustled the men against the wall, then out the doors and into their pods. I stood there stunned, my heart beating wildly, feeling stupid and lame. The guards ushered me out, and I drove home completely dejected. The next morning, I called into the jail and asked to speak with Willie.

He immediately began apologizing and then started to cry. "I'm so sorry, Roberto. It was my fault. I had it all planned with my homeboys. We were going to jump the Norteños. One of them insulted Stimy, and we don't take that lightly. We planned to fight them at the beginning of the study, but didn't do it out of respect for you. Man, I'm really sorry for what happened. That Bible study has been going through my mind all night. Mostly, I want to thank you for your prayer. That prayer stopped everything man."

"Prayer? What prayer?" I asked.

"You know, that prayer right at the end," he said.

"What do you mean it stopped everything?" I asked.

Willie told me that he had felt completely paralyzed, unable to move the moment that I finished praying.

I thought back to the night before and recalled that there had been no blows even though everyone had been ready to fight. I had walked right in between the two gangs to buzz for the guards. "Deliver us from evil" (*líbranos de mal)* had been my last words. I found Willie's explanation unbelievable, but intriguing. I told him that I didn't hold anything against him.

After hanging up, I called Pukie, who told me the same thing—that the Bible study had been in his head all night. Then he thanked me for the prayer that had stopped everything. This story, about how a pastor stopped a gang confrontation with a prayer, spread around the jail and then the larger Latino community. I am still struck by the power of God that was released through the closing words of the Lord's Prayer, a power that came in a time of need, extreme weakness, and desperate faith.

I have witnessed people publicly forgive longstanding enemies after being convicted by the Holy Spirit during Bible studies about loving our enemies. Inmates who were in a pod where nearly everyone was sick with the flu told me that after our Bible study and prayer for the flu to be eradicated from the pod in Jesus' name, everyone was better. I once led Bible studies among Maasai tribal people in a remote village in Southern Kenya near the border of Tanzania on John 10:1–18, the parable of the lost sheep, and how Jesus is the Good Shepherd and the door of the sheep pen. The Maasai people were suffering from a severe drought, and their cattle herds were at risk. The villagers attributed the rains that began soon after our gathering to the prayers we offered during those Bible studies.

Prophecy

Prophecy is a gift of the Spirit that involves receiving and giving specific, personal revelation from God. I once brought two friends from Canada and the UK into the Skagit County Jail. They had come to Tierra Nueva to teach a seminar on prophetic ministry.

After leading a dialogical Bible study with around twenty inmates, my friends asked if they could share some prophetic impressions. I sat in awe as they shared precise conditions that corresponded to the physical and psychological problems of the inmates in startling detail, sometimes including accurate information about how and when certain accidents had occurred. This created quite a stir among the men. My friends and I prayed for the men, and everyone claimed they received healing. Some of the men were crying. Others were laughing. Everyone expressed more serious interest in surrendering their life to Jesus.

After the study, I wondered why I hadn't been able to tune into these prophetic impressions. I felt deeply challenged to learn more about prophetic revelation as a life-transforming ministry. In the weeks following, I continued to debrief with inmates who had received their healing and some friends who had the gift of prophecy.

"Why am I so deaf to the voice of God regarding prophetic impressions when ministering in group settings?" I asked an experienced and gifted pastor.

"Have you ever judged someone for exercising prophetic gifts in public?" my friend asked. "Judging others who have exercised prophetic gifts in public can block you from moving in this gift publicly."

My friend's question and comment immediately brought up a childhood memory of attending a full Gospel businessmen's meeting with my dad. A speaker was exercising the gift of prophecy in a way that terrified me. I remembered watching in horror as he pointed to men in the audience whom he said were engaged in adulterous affairs. The feeling of shame in the room made me want to hide. I vowed never to return to those meetings. Over the years, I heard of "prophetic" words given about national events that seemed to correspond with partisan political agendas. As I recalled these memories, I felt moved to forgive the offenders who came to mind and to drop my judgments against them. In my prayer I gave the Holy Spirit permission to speak to me, giving me any revelation that could help me minister more personally. I continued to read books on hearing God's voice and the prophetic ministry, and I began to "earnestly desire the spiritual gifts, especially that I might prophesy," as Paul challenges his readers in 1 Corinthians 14:1.

Slowly I began to notice seemingly random impressions that would drop into my mind as thoughts or images. Once, while gathering with a small group of inmates in a visiting room, the words, "father wound," appeared in my consciousness. I felt stirred to share the phrase, so I said, "I recognize that we all have father wounds—but maybe this means something to someone here." To my surprise, one of the men looked at me, stunned, and then pulled up his shirt to reveal scars on his abdomen, where he had plunged a knife into his gut in a suicide attempt six months earlier. He shared how the desire to end his life had come from self-hatred because he had been beaten and verbally abused by his father. I shared about the importance of forgiveness, even in the absence of apologies, and the need to drop judgments in order to move forward in receiving healing. I was surprised by the man's eagerness to forgive his father. After gathering with the other inmates and praying for him, he announced that his chronic abdominal pain had just disappeared.

Often as I look at individuals, I see various images on the screen of my imagination: a metal bar coming down atop someone's head, a man's forehead breaking a windshield, or a knife in another's back. Sharing these God-given impressions ignites faith. When you share a prophetic word with someone, it can open them up to receiving prayer, or even to receiving Jesus!

Sometimes I unconsciously speak prophetically, such as when I give a hypothetical example of a situation. I might turn to someone on my right in a group and say, "Some people think that anyone who shows interest in reading the Bible when they're in a crisis is a hypocrite. They think that we need to prove we're serious about God when things are going well—not just in times of crisis. But then this guy gets caught cheating on his baby's mom, and now she wants nothing to do with him, and suddenly he's so desperate for God's help that he's willing to do anything." Then I might look at the next person around the circle and offer another seemingly random example. But then I notice that the individuals I've addressed are visibly moved, as if I've spoken directly into their personal life situations. As Paul describes in 1 Corinthians, prophesy can convict a person: "The secrets of his heart are disclosed, and so he will fall on his face and worship God, declaring that God is certainly among you" (14:24–25).

Since my earliest exposure to public prophecy involved shaming and the exposure of individual sin, I've found Paul's words in 1 Corinthians 14:3 to be an important reminder of the three primary purposes of prophesy: "edification and exhortation and consolation."

On one occasion, as I was moving around a circle of men praying silently, the thought came to me that I should tell a young man that he needn't worry about his daughter, that she would be okay. I ignored this thought, justifying my refusal to share because the man was quite young, and what if he didn't have a daughter? Finally I gave into the impression and whispered, "I think God wants you to know that you don't need to worry about your daughter—she's going to be okay." He dropped his head and cried, his head in his hands. The following week, he approached me, telling me that he was deeply moved by what I had shared, for at that very moment, he had been anguishing over the fact that his daughter's one-year birthday was the next day, and he was going to miss it.

"I knew that God was real and that he knew my pain," he told me. "That very night I gave my life over to Jesus."

When people discover that God not only knows their hidden pain, but also wants to encourage them with a very personal word, they feel compelled to draw closer to him.

In the midst of Bible study or during times of prayer, the Spirit can inspire specific words of encouragement or comfort to individuals. There are many ways to create an environment where people feel free to build each other up. One way is to invite people to join you in a short time of prayer, thanking God for things that come to mind for each person in the group. As people address God, prophetic words of encouragement often come quite naturally.

Distinguishing of Spirits

The gift of distinguishing of spirits is spiritual perception given by the Holy Spirit to help us identify demonic spirits or spiritual strongholds that are blocking people's understanding and spiritual growth as well as our efforts to communicate. Jesus names evil spirits in his ministry when he orders them to leave people. He casts out mute spirits (Mt 9:32–33), deaf and mute spirits (Mk 9:25), a spirit of infirmity (Lk 13:11), legion (Mk 5:9), and unclean spirits (Mt 12:43; Mk 1:23, 9:25; Lk 9:42, 11:24; Rev 18).

In the Gospel of John, Jesus distinguishes spirits with bold precision. "If you continue in my word, then you are truly disciples of mine; and you will know the truth and the truth will make you free," he tells a group of Jews who believe in him (Jn 8:31–32). But they refuse to acknowledge their enslavement, appealing to their racial-ethnic status as Abraham's descendants: "We are Abraham's descendants and have never yet been enslaved to anyone" (v. 33). Jesus presses them, "Truly, truly, I say to you, everyone who commits sin is the slave of sin" (v. 34). Discerning murderous intent in his listeners, Jesus names it, exposing a predatory spiritual power in the place that should be occupied by God: "I know that you are Abraham's offering; yet you seek to kill me, because my word has no place in you. I speak the things which I have seen with my Father; therefore you also do the things which you heard from your father" (vv. 37–38). When they appeal to Abraham as their father, Jesus names the one he sees enthroned in their hearts:

> You are of your father the devil, and you want to do the desires of your father. He was a murderer from the beginning, and does not stand in the truth because there is no truth in him. Whenever he speaks a lie, he speaks from his own nature, for he is a liar and the father of lies (v. 44).

When Jesus, the light of the world, exposes their hidden subjugation to the devil, the Jews confirm his discernment, blaspheming against him and labeling him as "Samaritan" and demon-possessed (v. 48). Then they pick up stones to throw at him, but Jesus hides himself and leaves the temple (v. 59).

Jesus also discerns spirits when his disciples, James and John, want to call down fire to consume the Samaritans who refuse hospitality to them when they are on their way to Jerusalem: "But He turned and rebuked them, and said, 'you do not know what kind of spirit you are of; for the Son of Man did not come to destroy men's lives, but to save them'" (Jn 9:55–56). Jesus discerns an evil spirit behind Peter's rebuke of him for foretelling his arrest, death and resurrection in Jerusalem, saying to him: "Get behind me, Satan! You are a stumbling block to me; for you are not setting your mind on God's interests, but man's." (Mt 16:23).

Jesus empowers his recruits to bind evil spirits (Mt 16:9, 18:18) and also to cast them out (Mt 10:1; Mk 6:7, 16:17; Lk 9:1). Jesus describes his role as binding the strong man so as to plunder his goods (Lk 11:20–22). He commissions his disciples clearly: "Behold, I have given you authority to tread on serpents and scorpions, and over all the power of the enemy, and nothing will injure you" (Lk 10:19).

Knowing how the enemy works will help us identify and counter spiritual assaults. Scripture warns us that the enemy accuses (Zec 3:1; Rev 12:10), tempts (Mk 1:13; 1 Cor 7:5), imprisons (Lk 13:16), thwarts (1 Thes 2:18), deceives (Jn 8:44; 2 Cor 11:14; 2 Jn 7), steals (Mt 13:19; Jn 10:10), and kills and destroys (Jn 10:10). Because many people hold to a blueprint theology, we need to recognize and teach how the enemy works so that people do not attribute the negative or destructive things that happen to themselves and others as from God or part of his sovereign will.[150] Jesus clearly teaches that it is not God's will for demons to afflict people. Predatory evil exists and must be deliberately countered through spiritual warfare.

When leading Bible studies in settings that are rife with accusation and shame, I often find it necessary to take authority over these things. In my opening prayer, I might say, "I silence accusation and shame in Jesus' name." In jails I sometimes declare the gathering space a "prosecutor-free zone in Jesus' name." People often comment that they notice immediate relief from blaming or shaming thoughts after these prayers.

Our first step is to discern which spirits are at work in individuals or groups. In some groups there may be religious spirits at work that hold people imprisoned to traditions. In other groups, tribalism, ethnic or racial pride, nationalism, party loyalties, or gang affiliations are at work. Hatred, depression, self-hatred, shame, racism, misogyny, misandry, pride, unbelief, and devotion to *Santa Muerte,*[151] witchcraft and occult practices, idolatries, and religious beliefs can block people's freedom to respond to Jesus.

Guerrilla Bible studies can include an invitation to conversion, a call to confession, the renunciation of evil, a declaration of forgiveness,

150. See Gregory Boyd, *Is God to Blame: Moving Beyond Pat Answers to the Problem of Suffering* (Downers Grove: InterVarsity Press, 2003).

151. *Santa Muerte* (Holy Death), short for *Nuestra Señora de la Santa Muerte* (Our Lady of Holy Death) is a female deity or folk saint that personifies death, venerated in Mexican and Mexican-American circles in the belief that it offers healing, protection and safe passage to the afterlife. Generally *Santa Muerte* appears as a skeletal female figure, clad in a long robe and holding one or more objects, usually a scythe and a globe. https://en.wikipedia.org/wiki/Santa_Muerte

and teaching about how sons and daughters of God can set themselves against evil spirits and cast them out with authority.

Various Kinds of Tongues

Various kinds of tongues are spiritual communications that can greatly enhance guerrilla Bible studies. In chapter six, we explored the connections between ceaseless prayer, praying in the Spirit, praying in tongues, and meditation on Scripture. We can pray in the Spirit and tongues as part of our preparation and also silently while we are ministering. Praying or worshipping in the Spirit is the most direct way our spirits can engage with the Holy Spirit, opening us to words of knowledge, words of wisdom, prophetic revelation, and spiritual discernment. All the gifts in the Spirit's arsenal inform our teaching and preaching.

Sometimes you or someone in the group may feel compelled to speak in tongues out loud. When tongues are spoken out loud, there should be an invitation for someone to exercise the gift of interpretation of tongues, as Paul suggests in his first epistle to the Corinthians: "Therefore let one who speaks in a tongue pray that he may interpret. . . Otherwise if you bless in the spirit only, how will the one who fills the place of the ungifted say the 'Amen' at your giving of thanks, since he does not know what you are saying?" (1 Cor 14:13, 16).

Interpretation of Tongues

The interpretation of tongues refers to interpreting the message spoken in a spiritual tongue into the language of the community.

A friend of mine, who is a pastor in France, told me how he came home late one night from a busy Sunday to find his wife ministering to an Ethiopian woman from Djibouti who spoke Somali and French. Though he was exhausted, he joined his wife in prayer. He was so tired he could barely think, and so he prayed aloud in tongues. The next morning the Ethiopian woman was surprised to learn that my friend didn't know a word of Somali. She recounted how shocked she was as he spoke about her and her family, sharing personal details that only God could know. She claims he prayed in flawless Somali—or so she heard, likely indicating that she herself was exercising the gift of interpreting tongues.

Additional Gifts in the Guerrilla Arsenal

In Romans 12, the Apostle Paul lists other gifts that can enhance our communication of the good news:

> Since we have gifts that differ according to the grace given to us, each of us is to exercise them accordingly: if prophecy, according to the proportion of his faith; if service, in his serving; or he who teaches, in his teaching; or he who exhorts, in his exhortation; he who gives, with liberality; he who leads, with diligence; he who shows mercy, with cheerfulness" (Rom 12:6–8).

Prophecy

The first gift on Paul's list in Romans 12 is prophesy, which we have already discussed at length above.[152]

Service

Paul names service (*diakonia*)[153] next. This gift refers to food distribution and serving (Lk 10:40; Jn 12:2; Acts 6:1) as well as supplying financial provision for Jesus' mission (Lk 8:3), for the poor (Acts 11:29; 2 Cor 8:4; 9:12–13), and for other ministries.[154] Jesus embodies the gift of service (*diakonia*) when he multiplies loaves for hungry crowds. He describes himself as coming not to be served but to serve (*diakoneo*), stating clearly, "I am among you as the one who serves" (Lk 22:27). His acts of service also include the giving of his life as a ransom (Mt 20:28; Mk 10:44).

In Acts, the apostles commission seven Greek-speaking men to serve Greek-speaking widows who are complaining that preference is being shown to Hebrew widows at the early church's equivalent of a food bank. The disciples say that these men need to be "full of the Spirit and wisdom" (Acts 6:3). Seven men are selected, and, "After praying, they laid their hands on them" (v. 6). As a result, "the word of God kept spreading;

152. This can be studied further with the help of many excellent books, such as Jordan Seng's chapter on prophesy in *Miracle Work*.

153. The early church commissioned deacons (1 Tm 3:10, 13) to accompany apostles (2 Cor 8:19).

154. See Acts 1:17; 6:4; 20:24; Rom 11:13; 2 Cor 5:18; Eph 4:12; 1 Tm 1:12; 2 Tm 4:5.

and the number of the disciples continued to increase greatly in Jerusalem, and a great many of the priests were becoming obedient to the faith" (v. 7).

The service of these first deacons appears to have been directly linked to the proclamation of the word. The first deacon, Stephen, is described as "full of grace and power . . . performing great wonders and signs among the people" (v. 8). Those who argue with him "were unable to cope with the wisdom and the Spirit with which he was speaking" (v. 10). Stephen preaches the longest sermon in the New Testament, for which he is martyred. Philip, the second deacon on the list, escapes the ensuing persecution by preaching Christ to a city in Samaria, where the people "heard and saw the signs that he was performing," including casting out unclean spirits and healing many who were paralyzed and lame (8:7). In the practice of the early Christians, concrete acts of service, mercy, wisdom, proclamation, deliverance, and healing all appear to flow together, and are often exercised by the same individuals.

Teaching

The spiritual gift of teaching builds up and empowers people. Teaching can happen under trees, in fields, prisons, cars, or in houses where drugs are sold. Anyone leading Bible studies recognizes the need to increase their effectiveness at helping people understand spiritual truths and knowing God's Word. Teaching is necessary at every stage in people's growth, from explaining basic truths about God and salvation to preparing people for baptism and outreach. We can learn to teach more effectively by studying empowering pedagogies and seeking to implement empowering practices. Recognizing teaching as a gift helps us position ourselves before God to receive. "You do not have because you do not ask," writes James (Jas 4:2). This gift of teaching can be "earnestly desired," as Paul exhorts in his first epistle to the Corinthians (14:1).

Exhorting

The word exhorting comes from the Greek, *parakaleo,* which means to call out (*kaleo*) from alongside (*para*). *Parakaleo* often means comfort in the Bible[155] and can refer either directly to God[156] or to humans (1 Cor 1:3–4). *Parakaleo* often means advocating or pleading,[157] as when a synagogue official advocates for Jesus to heal his daughter (Mk 5:23). People bring the sick (Mk 6:53) to Jesus and plead with him to lay hands on them (Mk 7:32) or touch them (Mk 8:22)—or for various apostles to come to them (Acts 9:38; 13:42; 16:9, 15). When we ask for Jesus to intervene, we are interceding for them. Advocacy done in Jesus' name brings miraculous results.

I regularly appeal to Jesus on behalf of the people with whom I'm reading the Bible. We regularly teach on prayer and invite people to ask God for help. Bible study participants witness many direct answers to these intercessions: a lost family member is found, an inmate has a successful day in court, an addicted partner chooses to enter a drug treatment program.

Advocacy at Tierra Nueva includes diverse actions on behalf of the people we meet in jail Bible studies, evening Psalms reading, our weekly worship service, or during Family Support Center office hours. We seek to discern the extent of our involvement through prayer and conversation on a case-by-case basis. We often see unusual breakthroughs that sometimes seem miraculous. We accompany people to criminal or immigration court, assist in posting bail, attend child custody hearings, or engage in petitions for clemency or forgiveness of debt or removal of bills from collection agencies. We witness the Holy Spirit's presence manifest through unusual favor, grace, forgiveness, and blessings. These happenings make the miracles in the Gospels suddenly seem possible even now, confirming the Word's authenticity.

Giving

The gift of giving also makes the good news of God's love powerfully real, bridging the divide between the haves and the have-nots in ways that reflect Kingdom of God economics. Once, after praying for a young

155. LXX Gn 26:67; 37:34; 38:12; 50:21; 2 Sm 12:24; 1 Chr 7:22; Is 40:1, 2.

156. LXX Ps 22:4; 70:21; 85:17; Is 40:11; 41:27; 49:10, 13; 51:3, 12; 57:18; 61:2; 66:12.

157. Mt 8:5, 34, 36; 18:29, 32; 26:53.

Mexican man named Jose during his deportation proceedings at a United States Immigration detention center and representing him in a bail reduction hearing, I received a call from a wealthy local businessman. He asked what I was doing and if I needed anything. Though Jose's bail had been reduced to $7500, it was still an impossible amount for him or us to cover. So I shared this with my friend, who immediately responded, "Well, if you believe in him, I will help!" Jose and I were both shocked when we bailed him out that afternoon. Eventually, we won his case and returned the money to Don with interest. On countless occasions, Gracie and I have received gifts of money that have enabled us to minister in impoverished places or to cover our own personal support needs.

Leading

Leading is another spiritual gift that is manifest socially. The Greek term, *proistēmi,* appears exclusively in Paul's writings and refers to people in positions of authority in the church.[158] Someone with the spiritual gift of leading is able to organize, direct, and mobilize people to accomplish God's mission in the world. Leadership requires great courage and strength. The spiritually gifted leader has a special charism to make things happen. The multiplication of leaders should be a continual priority for anyone leading guerrilla gospel encounters. Jesus himself instructed the seventy he commissioned for ministry to intercede for more workers: "The harvest is plentiful, but the laborers are few; therefore beseech the Lord of the harvest to send out laborers into his harvest" (Lk 10:2).

Showing Mercy

Showing mercy is a gift of the Holy Spirit that gets people's attention, inspiring similar actions. When someone who has been severely harmed by another chooses to forgive, the Kingdom of God becomes real. I once witnessed a man—who had scars crisscrossing his face, chest, and back from being cut up by two machete-wielding brothers in retaliation for an offense—publicly forgive those brothers several weeks after a Bible study on loving our enemies. The two brothers had approached one of our Honduran Tierra Nueva *promotores* (trainers), asking if the trainer

158. See 1 Thes 5:12; 1 Tm 3:4, 12; 5:17.

could serve as an intermediary between them and the man they'd cut. They wanted to ask publicly for his forgiveness. The man agreed to accept their apology and asked the brothers to forgive him for his offense as well. They spoke their apologies and forgiveness to one another, then embraced before the entire community, inspiring others to forgive their enemies!

The Manifold Grace of God

When any of the spiritual gifts are practiced with the anointing of the Holy Spirit, there will be clarification, conversion, and emotional and physical freedom.

May the stories in this chapter inspire your imagination about the possibilities that are available to us when the Holy Spirit confirms the truth of Scripture as it is discussed or proclaimed. May the Apostle Peter's words exhort us to practice the gifts of the Spirit for the glory of God:

> As each one has received a special gift, employ it in serving one another as good stewards of the manifold grace of God. Whoever speaks is to do so as one who is speaking the utterances of God; whoever serves is to do so as one who is serving by the strength which God supplies; so that in all things God may be glorified through Jesus Christ, to whom belongs the glory and dominion forever and ever. Amen. (1 Pt 4:10–11)

If guerrilla gospel encounters are to bring about conversion, healing, and personal and social transformation, we and those we read with regularly need to experience God's astounding grace and love.[159] May we all seek and find abundant provision for our journeys, drinking deeply of the living water that wells up to eternal life. May we find words to express the love of Christ in compelling ways that touch the hearts of the people we serve. May we witness the hearts of people with whom we read Scripture burn as the Spirit brings desperately needed relief. May we experience the joy of the harvest as people respond and enter with us into Jesus' Kingdom.

159. The Apostle Paul brilliantly emphasizes this in 1 Cor 13, a chapter that is sandwiched between his teachings on the gifts of the Spirit.

BIBLIOGRAPHY

Albright, W. F., *The Archaeology of Palestine*. Harmondsworth: Penguin, 1949.

Bevere, John. *Thus Saith the Lord: How to know when God is speaking to you through another*. Lake Mary: Creation House, 1999.

Bourgeault, Cynthia. *Centering Prayer and Inner Awakening*. Plymouth: Cowley, 2004.

Bourgeault, Cynthia. *The Heart of Centering Prayer: Nondual Christianity in Theory and Practice*. Boulder: Shambhala, 2016.

Bourguet, Daniel. *Méditation de la Bible*. Lyon: Olivetan, 2000.

Bourguet, Daniel. *The Tenderness of God*. Eugene: Cascade Books, 2017.

Branch, Robin Gallaher. *Six Biblical Plays for Contemporary Audiences*. Eugene: Cascade Books, 2016.

Brenton, Lancelot C. *The Septuagint with Apocrypha: Greek and English*. Grand Rapids: Zondervan, 1973.

Bristow, John T. *What Paul Really Said About Women: The Apostle's Liberating Views on Equality in Marriage, Leadership and Love*. New York: HarperCollins, 1988.

Boyd, Gregory A. *God at War: The Bible and Spiritual Conflict*. Downers Grove: InterVarsity, 1997.

Boyd, Gregory A. *Is God to Blame: Moving Beyond Pat Answers to the Problem of Suffering*. Downers Grove: InterVarsity Press, 2003.

Boyd, Gregory A. *Crucifixion of the Warrior God: Interpreting the Old Testament Violent Portraits of God in Light of the Cross*, 2 vols. Minneapolis: Fortress, 2017.

Brown, Raymond E. *The Gospel According to John (i–xii): Introduction, Translation, and Notes*. Garden City: Doubleday, 1966.

Ekblad, Bob. *Reading the Bible with the Damned*. Louisville: Westminster John Knox, 2005.

Ekblad, Bob. "Jesus' Surprising Offer of Living Cocaine: Contextual encounters at the well with Latino inmates in U.S. jails," in *Through the Eyes of Another: Intercultural Reading of the Bible*, ed. Hans de Wit, Louis Jonker, Marleen Kool, Daniel Schipani. Amsterdam: Vrije Universiteit, 2004, 133-136.

Ekblad, Bob. *A New Christian Manifesto: Pledging Allegiance to the Kingdom of God*. Louisville: Westminster John Knox, 2008.

Ekblad, Bob. "Reading Scripture for Good News Across Barriers of Race/Ethnicity, Class and Culture," *Multicultural Perspectives on Reading the Bible, Interpretation: A Journal of Bible and Theology* 65, no. 3 (July 2011), 229–248.

Ekblad, Bob. *The Beautiful Gate: Enter Jesus' Global Liberation Movement*. Burlington: The People's Seminary Press, 2017.

Fee, Gordon D. and Douglas Stewart, *How to Read the Bible for All Its Worth*. Grand Rapids: Zondervan, 1981.

Fee, Gordon D. *God's Empowering Presence: The Holy Spirit in the Letters of Paul*. Grand Rapids: Baker Academic, 1994.

Flood, Derek. *Disarming Scripture: Cherry-Picking Liberals, Violence-Loving Conservatives, and Why We All Need to Read the Bible Like Jesus Did* (San Francisco: Metanoia Books, 2014).

Guevara, Che. *Guerrilla Warfare, Guerrilla Tactics,* http://www3.uakron.edu/worldciv/pascher/che.html.

Holland, Joe and Peter Henriot, S.J., *Social Analysis: Linking Faith and Justice.* Maryknoll: Orbis, 1983.

Hutchison, John. *Our Lord's Signs in St. John's Gospel: Discussions Chiefly Exegetical and Doctrinal on the Eight Miracles in the Fourth Gospel.* Edinburgh, 1892.

Jersak, Brad. *Can You Hear Me? Tuning In to the God Who Speaks.* Abbotsford: Fresh Wind Press, 2003.

Jersak, Brad. Unpublished pamphlet, residential teaching seminar, Westminster Theological Centre. Telford, UK, September 2016.

Key dictionary of Greek, *Accordance Version 11.0.3,* November 2014

Louw, J. P. and Eugene Nida, eds., *Greek-English Lexicon of the New Testament,* Accordance Bible Software *Version 11.0.3* (November 2014).

Morris, Leon. *The Gospel According to John: The English Text with Introduction, Exposition and Notes.* Grand Rapids: Eerdmans, 1971.

Newbigin, Lesslie. *A Walk through the Bible.* Louisville: John Knox Press, 1999.

One Year Bible: The Entire English Standard Version in 365 Daily Readings (Wheaton: Tyndale, 1991).

Pacot, Simone. *Evangelizing the Depths.* Eugene: Cascade Books, 2018.

Pennington, Basil. *Centering Prayer: Renewing an Ancient Christian Prayer Form.* New York: Doubleday, 1980.

Peppiatt, Lucy. *Women and Worship at Corinth: Paul's Rhetorical Arguments in 1 Corinthians.* Eugene: Cascade Books, 2015.

Pitzele, Peter. *Scripture Windows: Towards a Practice of Bibliodrama.* Los Angeles: Torah Aurora Productions, 1998.

Sanford, Victoria. *Buried Secrets: Truth and Human Rights in Guatemala.* New York: Palgrave Macmillan, 2003.

Schlesinger, Stephen C., and Stephen Kinzer, *Bitter Fruit: The Untold Story of the American Coup in Guatemala.* New York: Doubleday, 1982.

Seng, Jordan. *Miracle Work: A Down-To-Earth Guide to Supernatural Ministries.* Downers Grove: IVP Books, 2013.

Stibbe, Mark. *Know Your Spiritual Gifts: How to Minister in the Power of the Spirit.* Grand Rapids: Zondervan, 1997.

Thayer, Joseph Henry. *Thayer's Greek-English Lexicon of the New Testament.* New York: Harper & Brothers, 1889. Accordance Bible Software.

Virkler, Mark and Patty. *Dialogue with God: Opening the Door to Two-Way Prayer.* Gainsville: Bridge-Logos, 1986.

Webb, William J. *Slaves, Women and Homosexuals: Exploring the Hermeneutics of Cultural Analysis.* Downers Grove: IVP Academic, 2001.

Werner, A., "The Galla of the East Africa Protectorate, Part II," in *Journal of the African Society,* no. 51, vol. 13 (April 1914).

West, Gerald O., *Contextual Bible Study.* Pietermaritzburg: Cluster, 1993.

West, Gerald O., "Matthew 20:1–15: An Ujamaa Centre Contextual Bible Study." http://ujamaa.ukzn.ac.za/Libraries/everything/matt20.sflb.ashx

Wilkinson, Gerald O. *Silence on the Mountain: Stories of Terror, Betrayal, and Forgetting in Guatemala.* Durham: Duke University Press, 2004.

24002052R00107

Made in the USA
Columbia, SC
17 August 2018